Permission to be Great

Increasing Engagement in Your School

Dan Butler

ConnectEDD Publishing
Chicago, Illinois

Praise for *Permission to be Great*

Dan Butler has written one of the most empowering, eclectic, and inspiring books I've read in a long time. Like your favorite mixtape or playlist, *Permission to be Great* contains a collection of timeless research, practitioner stories, and tools you'll want to come back to again and again.

    —Dr. Brad Gustafson
       National Distinguished Principal and Author

Education is a stressful profession. And the challenge of supporting and inspiring teachers who are burned out presses in on every school leader. But this challenge is met by Dan Butler in *Permission to be Great*. In this quick read, Butler offers authentic stories, practical strategies, and meaningful exercises to empower any educator committed to making a difference in their school.

    —Danny Steele
       Educator, Author, and Speaker

Dan blends appealing narratives with actionable information grounded in a solid research base to support leaders in creating high-energy, engaging learning cultures. He has sifted through a variety of strategies and tools to offer the reader what works best to build trust, positively engage staff, and support self-care; and his examples illustrate for the reader what this looks like in action. *Permission to Be Great* is an invitation to live and lead empowered, engaged, and energized. I read it cover-to-cover in one sitting!

    —Dana Schon, Ed.D.
       Professional Learning Director, School Administrators
       of Iowa

Educator engagement is an ongoing goal for schools. In *Permission to Be Great*, Dan Butler offers readers compelling stories, actionable steps, and models what great school communities can do to increase engagement.

—Peter DeWitt, Ed.D.
School Leadership Coach/Author/Facilitator

Dr. Dan Butler has hit the nail on the head with an issue currently threatening the educational community. *Permission to be Great* is immediately relevant to any educator struggling to meet the imbalance of demands of our constantly evolving educational system. Dan has written a compilation of beautiful and heart-wrenching stories to capture a true picture of burnout. Dan also includes strategies to engage a proactive approach to notice and name burnout behaviors. He makes the case for intentional approaches, such as prioritizing human connection, which are tried, true, and spoken from experience and from the heart. Dan gives practical ideas to help educators bring their best for students which can be put into practice today without a strain on the system's already lacking resources.

—Andrea Townsley
School Improvement Consultant, Grant Wood AEA,
former #IAedChat moderator

Two things impress me about Dan's work. First, his focus on "Permission." I cannot overstate its importance as a prerequisite of progress for any individual or group seeking to affect meaningful change. And second, his acknowledgement that everyone on staff has power and, therefore, everyone has a role to play in making a school great.

—Jamie Vollmer
Author of *Schools Cannot Do It Alone*

This book came along at exactly the right time. These days, when many of us are worried, off-balance, stressed, and disempowered, Dan shows us how to find balance, efficacy, positive energy, and authentic power.

Permission to be Great is a must-read book for anyone who wants to make a difference <u>and</u> live a good and beautiful life.

　　—Jim Knight
　　　Senior Partner of the Instructional
　　　Coaching Group & Author

After coaching hundreds of school leaders from around the world, I've noticed a trend: that school leaders are both their own biggest enemy as well as their own biggest opportunity. *Permission to be Great* shows you how to get out of your own way and focus on the latter. Taking action on Butler's ideas is your path toward sustainable greatness.

　　—Daniel Bauer
　　　Host of the *Better Leaders Better Schools* Podcast
　　　with over one million downloads

Permission to be Great is a resource for educators filled with practical advice and research-based strategies to avoid burnout, enhance communication, and seek the balance necessary to thrive in today's schools. Dan has eloquently woven stories from educators in the field, along with his own vulnerable mistakes and setbacks, to write a book that will become a go-to resource for readers.

　　—Jessica Cabeen
　　　National Distinguished Principal, Author, and Speaker

Each educational leader needs to create time – right now – to read this book from my colleague Dan Butler. Dan tackles the topic of how to empower leaders to be the agents for greatness they were designed to be. It reads like you and Dan are having a conversation over a cup of coffee, which in its own right is a challenging task for a writer. Dan provides idea after idea to inspire and excite school leaders to increase school engagement. As an avid reader of educational theory and practice, this text fits on the top shelf of my must-have resources.

— **Dr. Adam Drummond**
Associate Partner at the International Center for Leadership in Education & Author of *Instructional Change Agent:*
48 Ways to be the Leader Your School Needs

Dan does a great job of tackling the complex issue of teacher burnout in a very accessible manner. I found particular value in the fact that *Permission to be Great* speaks directly to the practitioner, but also speaks to those who lead and how to better care for those in their charge. I think all who read this book will find it engaging, easy to read, and PACKED with useful and well thought out tips for success.

— **PJ Caposey**
Superintendent of Schools, Meridian CUSD 223 (IL)
& Author

This is a must-read book for educators. Dan Butler addresses the real-world challenges in today's educational environment, and he provides a wealth of practical ideas and insights on how to respond to those challenges and increase your impact as a leader. *Permission to Be Great* is an inspiring and useful guide for what educational leaders can and should do to create an engaging and empowering school culture.

— **Tim Kight**
Founder and CEO of Focus 3

With practical and relevant information and suggestions to overcome the harsh challenges of educator burnout and subsequently improve a school's culture, *Permission to be Great* immediately engages the reader and provides timely assistance for all school leaders. Dr. Butler's unique style captures the reader's attention and highlights a growing need in America's

Schools. *Permission to be Great* challenges educators to take a hard look at the culture within their own buildings, while providing insightful and timely suggestions on ways to overcome those challenges. At a time when school leaders must dig deeper than ever before to positively impact the engagement of the educators in their buildings, Dr. Butler's book truly speaks to what it takes to understand and encourage educators to be at their best! Dan's book speaks to all of us who are educators, have been educators, or have struggled with the challenges of leading buildings and/or districts. From the opening chapter, *Permission to be Great* engages the reader and provides timely and beneficial information on improving a school's culture from the roots of the organization—the educators!

—Dr. Tim Gilson
Associate Professor of Educational Psychology, Foundations, and Leadership Studies, University of Northern Iowa

Dan Butler's *Permission to be Great* provides an organized and practical approach to identifying educator burnout and making effective changes in the school or district in which it occurs. These researched based, practical approaches can easily be implemented into the environment quickly and effectively. Dr. Butler's *Permission to be Great* addresses the teacher and administration with compassion, empathy, and the proper wordsmithing to engage the reader to act immediately and make a difference in the world around them. In the line of work I am in, I see it to be so essential to address the self-care and brain health of the adult staff first before tending to the needs of the students they serve. Dr. Butler pens a no hitter in identifying how to best match our educators to hit a home run for the students in our future.

—Molly Schreiber, MS E-RYT 500
**Founder and CEO of Challenge to Change, Inc.
Social and Emotional Learning Through Yoga
and Mindfulness**

Permission to be Great moves you from *wanting* to be the best version of yourself to *working* to be the best version of yourself. If you are looking for quick fixes and easy solutions to being great, put this down and continue spinning your wheels. If you are looking to roll your sleeves up and do the right work to be the leader you deserve to be, here is your permission.

— **Kelly Simon**
Director of Curriculum, Instruction, and Assessment:
Western Dubuque Schools

Permission to be Great provides leaders with the opportunity to be just that...great. The stories will engage you; the process will force you to reflect; and the practical application of the models will yield immediate results. The identification of burnout practices and strategies to extinguish those practices will help you lead in whatever role you currently serve. I highly recommend picking up a copy and giving yourself and your team permission to be great.

— **Joe Sanfelippo**
Superintendent of Fall Creek Schools, Wisconsin, Author,
and Speaker

In *Permission to be Great*, Dan Butler not only tackles the "Why?" behind educator burnout but delivers strategies to combat it. Educators and leaders alike will be equipped with real world tools, ideas, and strategies to increase engagement and lead boldly.

— **Greg Deutmeyer**
Instructional Coach and Founder/Co-Host of the
Instructional Coaching Corner Podcast

Permission to be Great is the permission slip educators need. Dan normalizes common feelings, struggles, and obstacles that educators face daily and then offers impactful strategies that lead to connection, well-being, and increased engagement.

—Sanée Bell
Author of *Be Excellent on Purpose: Intentional Strategies for Impactful Leadership*

WOW! In an age of TikTok, Ted Talks, and social media where the spotlight is shining on the individual, Dan Butler gives us all *Permission to be Great*! What I love is that in reading *Permission to be Great* you can't help but feel like Dan is sitting next to you and you are having a conversation. Dan puts the emphasis on people. Too many leaders lose sight of what is truly important: people. If you want to take your leadership to the next level, don't hesitate in diving into this book. I promise, it will Give YOU the permission to be great!

—**Ben Gilpin**
Principal, Author, and Speaker

This publication is available at discount pricing when purchased in quantity for educational purposes, promotions, or fundraisers. For inquiries and details, contact the publisher at:

info@connecteddpublishing.com

Published by ConnectEDD Publishing LLC, Chicago, IL
www.connecteddpublishing.com

Cover Design: Kheila Dunkerly

Permission to be Great: Increasing Engagement in Your School/ Dan Butler. —1st ed.
Paperback ISBN 978-1-7361996-3-3

Dedication

Professionally, this book is dedicated to every educator that I have had the pleasure of working with in my career. Education is the most important profession in the world and we need you now more than ever. Thank you for pouring your heart and soul into all that you do.

Personally, this book is dedicated to my wife and best friend, Johna, and my two boys, Mason and Nolan. You have been an incredible support and continue to be the best. Your unwavering encouragement and inspiration allowed me to prevent burnout, while writing a book about it. I could not have done this without you; I love you so much.

Permission to be Great

Increasing Engagement in Your School

Table of Contents

Introduction

"Man often becomes what he believes himself to be. If I keep on saying to myself that I cannot do a certain thing, it is possible that I may end by really becoming incapable of doing it. On the contrary, if I have the belief that I can do it, I shall surely acquire the capacity to do it, even if I may not have it at the beginning."

Mahatma Gandhi

I was walking through the doors of John F. Kennedy Elementary School on a mild June afternoon finishing my final day of fourth grade. For the first time in my brief school career, I did not want the year to end. I was a mediocre student at best and did not dedicate the time or effort necessary to improving. I lacked confidence, struggled mightily comprehending anything I read, and just did not seem to connect with school. I loved seeing my friends, playing at recess, and participating in physical education; nonetheless, the academic content in the classroom was a completely different story. When it was time to read, I could not understand why my friends could recall everything from the text, while I did not comprehend a thing. My previous teachers were less than patient and undoubtedly annoyed with my struggles. The leading intervention strategy at the time was, "If it doesn't make sense, Dan, read it again." I would read passage after passage with a high level of accuracy and end up in the same place—not understanding anything.

1

Not only was I frustrated with my unsuccessful attempts at reading; my teachers were equally frustrated. I have an older brother who excelled in school and did not need to put forth much effort to be successful. We had many of the same teachers over the years and I will never forget a parent/teacher conference I attended with my mom in elementary school nearly thirty years ago. My teacher sat down with my mother and me to go over progress reports, share some of my projects, and go through the typical parent/teacher conference protocol. Near the end of the conference, my teacher made a comment that has stuck with me for nearly three decades, grumbling, "You know, Dan isn't nearly as smart as his brother, Sam." Not all my memories from elementary school are like this one, but needless to say, my struggle was real.

Fourth grade was completely different because of an amazing human being, someone who went above and beyond the call of duty. Mrs. Lammers exhibited an incredible belief in me and made me want to learn more each day. She showed me that mistakes are not fatal, reading *Sports Illustrated for Kids* is completely acceptable if it piques your interest, and intelligence is not fixed; rather, success will come to those who work hard and follow their passions. I loved Mrs. Lammers for many reasons: her affection for baseball, the way that she brought characters to life when she read *Tales of a Fourth Grade Nothing*, and, most importantly, how she made an intentional effort to connect with me while pushing me toward inconceivably higher levels.

As we were heading through the halls toward the exit door on that June afternoon, Mrs. Lammers asked about my plans for summer, inquired whether I really thought the Oakland A's would repeat as World Series champions in the fall, and reassured me that fifth grade wasn't all that scary. Approaching the exterior door, steps away from three months of freedom, Mrs. Lammers put her arm on my shoulder, turned me around to look deep into her brown eyes and said, "Dan Butler, you have my full permission to be great."

Those words have stuck with me since my teacher first uttered them at the end of the 1989-1990 school year. At the time, I did not think much of this interaction, other than considering Mrs. Lammers to be pretty darn cool. As I have grown as an educator, working with students and adults in a field where we have tremendous influence over others, I have come to appreciate her words more than ever. We work in a system in which there is no shortage of school improvement efforts and initiatives and the pressure to improve is ever present. I am a firm believer in school improvement and constantly search for ways to get better; however, I have come to realize that many times we overthink it.

Whether we are talking about 1989 or 2035, education was and always will be about people. Making genuine human connections among the people we serve and with whom we serve has been and will be the key accelerator in our school improvement efforts. I am not discounting comprehensive systems and programs that schools across the globe are implementing to better serve students, but we must never lose sight of establishing strong, authentic relationships with our students, families, and colleagues. In education, common sense often gets trumped by common practice. Many times all it takes for the conditions to be ripe for greatness is being given the permission to be great.

> In education, common sense often gets trumped by common practice.

How to Use
Permission to be Great

In this book, I will provide practical insights to empower leaders to create systems of positive energy, involvement, efficacy, and engagement. Please note, however, that I define "leader" as anyone who positively influences others and motivates them to be better. It does not matter to me if you are a paraprofessional, school secretary, teacher, assistant principal, food service worker, superintendent, bus driver, school counselor, instructional coach, principal, or custodian. You have the ability to lead and can benefit from this content.

Because everyone in the school setting can build skill from the content provided in this book, this was written for all educators, including current school leaders and aspiring school leaders who desire to make the workplace more engaging for not only themselves, but also for those they serve. As a building principal who has spent a great deal of time in the university setting completing master's, specialist's, and doctoral degrees in educational leadership, I also wrote this book for universities to use when preparing educators to excel in the role of school administrator. Educator burnout and workplace engagement are certainly popular topics within the educational community and there are excellent books on the market that address these issues. However, few, if any, offer the blend of research, practical experiences from the field, and

5

systematic approaches to create schools filled with vigor, collaboration, and effectiveness provided in this book.

This book is laden with success stories, current research, proven leadership practices, engagement enhancers, and self-care strategies designed to create an environment for your classroom, school, or district to thrive. In addition to the introduction and conclusion, it is organized into five chapters.

In chapter 1, I provide a definition of educator burnout and the three dimensions of emotional exhaustion, depersonalization, and personal accomplishment. I also describe six mismatches between educators and the work environment that contribute to burnout. Within these mismatches, I introduce some of the current struggles educators face and provide a preview of how to combat this phenomenon. The chapter concludes by sharing some of the financial, physical, and social consequences of educator burnout.

Chapters 2-5 dig deeper into the distinct mismatches between school employees and the work environment including workload; control, and autonomy; encouragement, recognition, and appreciation; building community and relationships; and promoting fairness through the establishment of core values. By finding better fits within these areas of work, leaders will increase engagement in schools, while extinguishing educator burnout. Chapters 2-5 also include the following components:

1. **Stories from the Field:** Each chapter begins with success stories shared from a collection of students, educators, and families I have encountered throughout the course of my leadership journey.

2. **Practical Research, Leadership Practices, and Experiences:** Here you will find excerpts from easily understandable research findings, as well as effective practices and my personal experiences to solidify the content being presented.

3. **Engagement Enhancers:** At the end of these chapters, you will find four simple and impactful ideas that can be implemented within your school or district. Research from Lyubomirsky (2008) suggests roughly 40% of our well-being is rooted in intentional activity. With this knowledge at our disposal, it is critical to find the right strategies and tactics to boost our levels of engagement. These *Engagement Enhancers* are designed to be easily executed and it is my hope that after you read about them today, you will have the ability to put them into place tomorrow.

4. **Caring for You:** Being in a service position, such as education, requires countless hours tending to the needs of others. Educators experience a wide range of emotions and suppressing those emotions does not typically work well. To conclude these chapters, two self-care strategies are described that align with the concepts of each chapter. I define "self-care" as activities we do intentionally to cultivate our physical, mental, and emotional health. Many times self-care is associated with massages, bubble baths, face masks, and other extravagant measures. The eight tactics in these chapters do not fall into this category. They are simple, yet effective. When we invest time in caring for ourselves, we have the energy and enthusiasm to care for those we lead.

Thank you for embarking on this journey with me to learn more about the beliefs, behaviors, skills, and mindsets to diminish workplace burnout and increase educator engagement. As you read this book, it is my sincere hope that you become more passionate about your work, while obtaining useful tools to provide you and the people you serve *Permission to be Great.*

CHAPTER 1

The Problem

"We are what we repeatedly do. Excellence then, is not an act, but a habit."

Aristotle

Steve has been teaching for ten years in the same high-performing suburban district. He is considered a leader among his colleagues, a dedicated professional, and many families request to have him as their child's teacher each year. In the last several weeks, Steve has been struggling. He consistently stays at school until 7:00 each evening after meeting with overbearing parents, serving on a literacy committee, coaching swimming, grading papers, designing appropriate learning accommodations, and planning engaging virtual lessons for his students learning at home during the COVID-19 pandemic. As Steve goes through this routine repeatedly without ample time to recover, he becomes incredibly fatigued. He comes home to crash and wakes up in the morning distraught about having to do it all over again. The more demands being placed on Steve, the more exhausted he becomes, which causes him to withdraw from different groups at school. Typically, he ate lunch in the staff lounge, while enjoying the company of his colleagues, and participated in staff functions outside the school day. Now, he just does not have the energy or enthusiasm to join in. Additionally, Steve has become short tempered with his students and is losing his sense of confidence. He feels as though he is no longer making a difference.

Maria is entering her third year as an instructional coach at Taft Middle School. Taft is reasonably small, with three hundred students in sixth, seventh, and eighth grades. In recent years, it has been recognized at the state level for high achievement on standardized assessment measures. Prior to this assignment, Maria served as a science teacher for twenty-one years in a low-income high school. In addition to her responsibilities as an instructional coach, she loves working with students who are disadvantaged and finds great joy in locating and allocating resources to help with the increasing social and emotional needs of kids and their families. Colleagues and administrators Maria worked with in the past praised her ability to connect with hard-to-reach students. Initially, Maria loved her job as an instructional coach, but over the past year or so, she has really struggled trying to navigate the culture of Taft. While this building achieves at high levels in terms of standardized assessments, she believes they are failing miserably to meet the unique learning needs of many students. Maria believes this is due to required, inflexible pedagogy and mandated curricular materials with limited teacher choice. The policies and practices at Taft focus solely on academic achievement, while neglecting the ever present and increasing social and emotional needs of students. In addition, Maria is rarely acknowledged by her administrator and really has no idea if she is even doing a good job. She feels as though she no longer matters. Kids may be nailing the standardized tests at Taft, but they are falling apart emotionally, and Maria just cannot take it anymore.

Do either of these scenarios sound familiar? Can you relate to them? While the stories of Steve and Maria are different, they share a common thread: both professionals experience painful conflicts with certain aspects of their jobs and are on the verge of experiencing educator burnout. As depressing as their experiences may sound, they are not unlike the current reality many other educators experience each day. Teaching is tough every single day and dedicated educators are doing all they can to stay afloat. Eventually, this begins taking a toll—professionally, personally, or both.

Educators like Steve and Maria are under constant pressure to meet the needs of a variety of learners, engage families, and collaborate with colleagues, while doing everything necessary to make a positive difference in the lives of students. These, among a myriad of other responsibilities, are part of the typical routine in the life of an educator in the twenty-first century. With so much being demanded of educators without an extra minute added to the school day, educators in all roles are at a higher-than-ever risk to experience burnout.

The concept of educator burnout has gained the attention of researchers in the past fifty years, particularly in the last twenty. In fact, the phenomenon has been described as the biggest occupational hazard of the 21st century. Recognized authorities Christina Maslach and Michael Leiter (1997), define burnout as a psychological syndrome consisting of a state of emotional exhaustion in which one is cynical about the value of one's occupation and doubtful about one's ability to perform. Emotional exhaustion, cynicism, and low efficacy are the three dimensions of burnout in the workplace context. Educators experiencing emotional exhaustion feel overextended by their work and simply depleted. Those who become cynical adopt an impersonal approach to their work and withdraw from students, colleagues, families, or members of the school community. Finally, educators with low efficacy lose confidence in themselves and the belief that they can make a difference.

There are many contributing factors to workplace burnout, though the research literature has identified the primary causes as six recurring mismatches between people and their work environment. Research studies suggest its prevalence may be on the rise, due to many factors, including work overload, a lack of autonomy, insufficient encouragement, recognition, or appreciation, depleted relationships, lack of fairness, and value conflicts (Maslach, et al., 2001). The greater the mismatch between each area of the school setting and the educator, the greater the risk of burnout. Conversely, the greater the match, the better the chances of workplace engagement. Extinguishing burnout means finding a better fit between people and their work. Let's take a look at the six recurring mismatches in the next several sections.

Workload

Having too much to do and insufficient time or resources to do it is a legitimate issue. In addition to the many demands and responsibilities placed upon educators, 24/7 accessibility and the hyper-connected environment in which educators work today presents another set of issues related to work overload. With access to email, grade books, lesson plans, text messages, social media, and instructional resources at the click of a mouse or touchscreen, it is more difficult than ever to disconnect from work obligations. The boundary lines between work and life responsibilities have been blurred with the advancement of technology, and if educators are not intentional about separating the two, the work never seems to end.

"Workload" refers to the amount of work to be done in a given time with a finite amount of resources. Increased educator demands, such as larger class sizes, mandatory initiatives, and accountability procedures with decreased resources, including fewer staff, less instructional time, and limited leadership, contribute to burnout. Like Steve, when this level of workload becomes the norm and there is little opportunity to rest, recover, and restore balance, job burnout is inevitable.

Since 1990, more than thirty-two curricular areas, programs, and federal or local initiatives have been added to the plates of instructors in the United States (Vollmer, 2010). Some examples of these programs have included conflict/peer resolution, at risk/dropout prevention, personal financial literacy, trauma-informed care, Positive Behavioral Interventions and Support (PBIS), and the Early Literacy Initiative, to name a few. In addition to this initiative and curricular overload, not one minute has been added to the instructional day in six decades.

Twenty-first century educators are faced with more demands than educators in any previous era. They are often expected to act as social workers, health care providers, and even parents, while continuing to educate children about core content areas, technology, and the global community. As a result of these pressures, many educators are leaving the profession, suffering the consequences of job-related stress and depleted engagement.

Control and Autonomy

When educators feel micromanaged and believe they do not have a voice in what they do, they are much more susceptible to burnout. According to Gallup's State of America's Schools 2013 report, teachers rank last in all surveyed occupational groups in terms of their likelihood to say their opinions seem to count at work. On the contrary, when control is present, educators can participate in important decisions about work, solve problems, and contribute to the fulfillment of responsibilities, all while experiencing autonomy. Moreover, employees who have the perceived capacity to influence decisions that affect their work, exercise professional judgment, and gain access to necessary resources are more likely to experience job engagement, which is the positive antithesis of job burnout (Maslach, et al., 2001). High-stakes accountability measures, teacher evaluations tied to student performance, standardization of instruction, reduced funding, disconnected professional learning, intensive, prescriptive curriculum pacing guides, and micromanagement from leadership are some of the recent trends that threaten educator autonomy and contribute to burnout. Simply stated, one way to promote engagement is to allow educators more control and autonomy.

Encouragement, Recognition, and Appreciation (ERA)

I love baseball and throughout this book you will encounter a few stories related to this passion of mine. In baseball, a lower earned run average (or ERA) is a good thing, as this is an indicator of the number of runs for which a pitcher is responsible and a reliable statistic to measure pitching performance. When referring to school leadership, it is exactly the opposite and best to have as high an ERA (Encouragement, Recognition, and Appreciation) as possible. Encouragement, recognition, and appreciation includes the financial and social acknowledgement one receives for contributions on the job consistent with expectations. Examples of ERA include praise, awards, supportive feedback, perks, acknowledgement, and salary. These examples are designed to recognize and reinforce positive behavior. While financial compensation is necessary and awards are nice, research from Chapman and White (2019) has shown that the everyday appreciation workers receive is even more valuable. The number one factor in job satisfaction is not the amount of pay received, but whether people feel appreciated and valued for the work they do. On the other hand, when encouragement, recognition, and appreciation are absent, as in Maria's situation, there is a strong likelihood of an employee heading down the road to disengagement, burnout, and inefficacy. People want to be acknowledged and know that what they think, say, and do matters. As you work through the content of this book, you will discover a multitude of examples designed to boost ERA in the school setting.

Community and Relationships

The fourth mismatch between employees and the work environment occurs when people lose a sense of positive connection with others in the workplace. Positive relationships serve as the foundation upon which everything is built in education. At the end of the day, it is not about plans, it is not about procedures, it is not about programs; it is always about people (Whitaker, 2020). The stronger the established relationships, the stronger the community, and the more engagement in schools. Educators like Steve and Maria are susceptible to burnout when they lose a sense of positive connection with others in their schools or districts. Insensitive coworkers and colleagues may be stressors, due to discourtesy or even bullying. Cliques in schools tend to thrive and relationships deflate when opinions of others are belittled, shame occurs in a public manner, access to social opportunities is denied or withheld, or information is limited to certain groups. Unfortunately, these behaviors occur in schools and such behaviors are a recipe for disengagement, toxicity, ineffectiveness, and burnout. Inversely, coworkers, colleagues, and supervisors can be critical resources for providing support, trust, and friendship. People thrive in a community and function best when they share praise, comfort, and happiness, establishing an atmosphere of affection and respect for each other. The experiences that contribute to well-being are often amplified through positive relationships and can give life purpose and meaning, which is associated with increased confidence, greater engagement, and decreased burnout (Seligman, 2011). This book is filled with relationship and community building strategies that I have seen work at schools in which I have served.

Fairness

People want to be treated in a consistent manner that aligns with their expectations and values. Fairness is the extent to which decisions at work are perceived as being reasonable and equitable. Cynicism, anger, and hostility are likely to arise when people feel they are not treated with an appropriate level of respect. Fairness is about how people are treated in comparison to others. Fairness communicates reverence and confirms self-worth. When decision making is perceived as unfair, engagement of educators deteriorates. Furthermore, when trust between administrators and teachers is diminished, burnout is heightened and, left unchecked, inescapable. As you continue reading, you will find ideas for ensuring that everyone with whom you interact is treated fairly and respectfully through the establishment of core values.

Values

Over the course of my career in education, I have been to more meetings than I can count. I suspect you can relate. At some of these meetings, we have engaged in healthy debates related to change initiatives, new curriculum, budget cuts, and so forth. As I reflect on these debates with my colleagues, I recall this oft-repeated phrase: "Well, I guess we can go that route, because I won't die on that hill." This is an expression that originates from the military and refers to an issue the group would like to address, but, in the end, might be too much of a hassle to actually undertake. Now, when I hear that expression in leadership meetings, even with my own staff, I flip it around, asking, "What hill *are* you willing to die on?" By asking that question, I am looking for something that is non-negotiable, something you stand for, something in which you believe to your core. Your values.

Values are the ideals and motivations that originally attracted people to their job. When there is a conflict on the job and a gap between individual and organizational values, employees—like Maria—will find themselves making a trade-off between work they *want to do* and work they *have to do* which can contribute to greater burnout (Maslach & Leiter, 2016). The term "job fit" is used often when discussing personnel. This is all about a match of individual and organizational values. The stronger the fit between the individual and the school/district, the higher the level of engagement. On the other side of that coin, the weaker the fit, the more likely it will result in job burnout.

Why Should We Care?

As part of the 2013 *State of America's Schools* report, Gallup reported that only 31% of teachers in the United States are engaged in their work, meaning less than 1/3 of surveyed educators indicated high levels of energy, involvement, and efficacy while at school. Additionally, 56% of teachers reported being not engaged, suggesting they were not necessarily causing issues, but not lighting the world on fire either. Teachers in this category can adequately be described as showing up and essentially going through the motions. Conclusively, 13% of these teachers reported being actively disengaged in their positions. These teachers are not only unhappy, but also openly derailing the performance of others. Chew on these statistics for a minute. Roughly 70% of teachers in the United States are either going through the motions or intentionally disrupting the improvement efforts of their schools. To say this is concerning on many levels would be a drastic understatement. Educators who do not love their work are certainly not bringing their best to students and the financial, physical, and social consequences of that are very real.

Financial Implications

Educator burnout is threatening the well-being of society, negatively impacting not only the optimal growth of students, but also our educational system overall. Ultimately, it results in a negative financial impact as well. Teacher attrition due to work stress is increasing, with 40-50% of new teachers leaving the profession after only three years of service. In addition, between 8-15% of teachers overall are leaving the profession every year (Ingersoll et al., 2018). Research has shown a lack of administrative support, increased demands, tenuous relations with parents, and limited autonomy as the main sources of work stress contributing to the three dimensions of burnout. Stressors that educators regularly encounter include role overload, disruptive students, non-supportive or over involved parents, poor relationships with colleagues, evaluation, high-stakes testing, negotiation battles, and accountability in which job security is threatened (Steinhardt et al., 2011).

When top-quality educators are burned out, absentee rates rise, meaning more substitutes, less consistency and predictability, and decreased levels of student learning. Additionally, the social dynamics of work have changed in the last twenty years, as organizations have increasingly focused on results (like Maria's middle school) to the detriment of employees' well-being. Supporting this claim, Pfeffer (2018), contends, "The workplace profoundly affects human health and mortality, and too many workplaces are harmful to people's health; people are literally dying for a paycheck" (p. 8). Job stress costs the United States economy an estimated $300 billion annually in sick leave, long-term disability, and excessive job turnover (Medina, 2014). Conclusively, a pilot study conducted by Barnes et al. (2007) determined teacher turnover costs taxpayers $7.3 billion each year.

Physical Outcomes

In addition to the financial burden the burnout phenomenon presents, there are several negative physical consequences to educators, including sleep disturbances, physical tension in the body, anxiety, gastro-intestinal disorders, depression, and the development of poor nutritional habits. Furthermore, physical illness, increased feelings of hopelessness, irritability, impatience, and poor interpersonal relationships with family, coworkers, and students are common experiences for the educator experiencing burnout. Disengaged, unhealthy, and unhappy educators are not as productive, innovative, energetic, or effective, which ultimately leads to lower levels of student achievement (Arens & Morin, 2016). More importantly, educators who experience burnout lose the joy and fulfillment of making a difference in the lives of students (Leiter & Maslach, 2005).

Social Consequences

Social consequences also arise in the school setting because of burnout. When educators are burned out, they may withdraw, which can put a strain on relationships and lead to incivility. Goleman (2006) explains that behavior is contagious: "Like secondhand smoke, the leakage of emotions can make an innocent bystander a casualty of someone else's toxic state" (p. 14). Christakis and Fowler (2011) expand on this notion and describe the phenomenon as "emotional contagion." They assert that a person's moods are affected by the emotional states of people with whom they interact. People are hardwired to mimic others outwardly and come to adopt their inward states. This can become problematic in the work context, as one person having a sense of low morale and disengagement can impact an organization negatively. When these feelings ripple out to others within the work group, it is a recipe for dysfunction. Fortunately, positive emotions are also contagious and can affect the work situation in a productive manner (Fredrickson, 2009). Many of the ideas and practices discussed in this book are geared toward boosting positive emotions in the school setting.

While the evidence related to the negative consequences of burnout is overwhelming and very real, the good news is, it does not have to be this way. With intentional approaches and relatively simple tactics, leaders can extinguish burnout and promote engagement in their school settings. Over the course of the next four chapters, I will walk you through how to do this, while sharing success stories, proven leadership practices, engagement enhancers, and self-care strategies that will allow you to lead your school or district toward positive change. The six mismatches between educator and school context will be addressed in four chapters to initiate higher levels of energy, involvement, and efficacy in the people you serve. Now that you know the truth about burnout, let's get on the path toward engagement. You have my full permission to be great.

CHAPTER 2

Balancing Workload, Control, and Autonomy

"Challenges are what makes life interesting and overcoming them is what makes life meaningful."

Joshua J. Marine

It was 4:00 a.m. and Marcus slowly awoke in an unusual location, faced with fluorescent lights blinding his vision. A nurse entered the room as he tried to sit upright. Marcus started to sweat, wondering what in the world he was doing in a hospital. The nurse noticed the confused look on his face and told him he had been in an accident the night before.

Marcus was stiff and sore from sleeping on a hospital bed, but could walk without difficulty. After washing his hands and splashing water on his face in the restroom, he glanced above the sink to see absolute horror confronting him in the mirror. The left side of his face was destroyed. More than ten stitches lined his left eyebrow, abrasions painted the left canvas of his face, and bruises were starting to form along his cheek and jaw bones.

Marcus was attending a professional conference and had the opportunity to facilitate two sessions related to equity and, oddly enough, promoting self-care for leaders. In addition to attending and presenting at this conference, he was scrambling to wrap up the school year as a high school principal in his Title 1 building, while simultaneously preparing for the next. Additionally, he was serving as an adjunct professor at a local university, coaching his daughters in summer basketball, organizing the research study for his doctoral dissertation—and failing miserably to keep it all together.

Burnout Behavior: Wearing Busyness Like a Badge of Honor.
Can you relate to the following exchange heard in a typical school hallway between two teachers?

"How are you?"

"I'm SO BUSY!"

It's like a default setting that we respond and celebrate how busy we are, as if there were a scoreboard. There is a misunderstanding in our society that being busy is equivalent to being productive, purposeful, and effective. In no way, shape, or form am I saying that the days of educators aren't full. They are; it's real. Rather than celebrating our busyness, however, let's celebrate our purpose and effectiveness.

While countless opportunities were provided to Marcus, his inability to say "No" was leading to unmanageable demands, and his physical and mental health were deteriorating. At a time when he should have been extraordinarily grateful for the opportunities provided to him, he was overweight, overextended emotionally, cynical, and questioning his leadership competence, as he failed to establish any semblance of stability.

The night of the accident, Marcus was having dinner with a few principal colleagues and when it was time to head back to the hotel, he decided to hop on an electric scooter for an easy trip home—or so he thought. He did not remember much about this trip, other than getting knocked off course by some loose pavement which sent him flying over a curb and landing directly on the left side of his face. After that, everything was a blank in his mind and stayed that way until he awoke the next morning.

After making an emotional call to his wife letting her know he was OK and would be flying out later that afternoon, Marcus began to reflect on this situation. He could have easily died as a result of the accident. As he was experiencing these emotions, he realized that he needed to slow his life down, because if he didn't, he was going to drive himself to an early grave. This may sound dramatic; nonetheless, the scenario hit him right between the eyes, figuratively and literally. Marcus was moving too fast, taking on too much, not caring for himself, and changes needed to occur.

While extremely painful (physically and emotionally), this was the wakeup call Marcus needed. With the intense demands placed on educators in the twenty-first century, we can go down a dark path, potentially leaving us alone in an unknown emergency room if we are not intentional with our choices. More than ever, it is critical to invest in yourself so you can better invest in others. Extinguishing burnout while increasing engagement requires a systematic effort that goes beyond the individual. If leaders are interested in improving their systems, while increasing the well-being of the people they lead, they must first make a commitment to managing their workload demands.

The Mismatch

If you are working in a school, odds are good that you cannot possibly meet all the demands thrust upon you on any given day. Designing interventions for kids who struggle, facilitating formative assessments for the lesson that was just delivered, answering emails from concerned parents, leading professional learning, updating digital content for virtual learners, and so on and so forth. At every school I visit, there are simply too many demands and not enough resources to meet those demands.

Burnout researchers, Bakker and Demerouti (2007), developed the *Job Demands-Resources* model which posits all work activities can be placed into one of two categories: Demands or Resources. In addition to the demands mentioned above, others include lesson planning, mandatory training, standardized assessments, serving on building committees, school board meetings, grading and providing feedback, and student discipline, to name a few. And with the advent of a global pandemic, we can now add virtual teaching and contact tracing as additional demands. When there is an imbalance between the demands we face and the amount of resources available to meet those demands, burnout is likely to occur. Conversely, when there are adequate resources, such as time, social support, role clarity, and effective leadership to meet the work demands, job engagement is much more likely. Similar to Maslach, et al. (2001), I view engagement as the positive antithesis of burnout.

Unfortunately, the demands placed upon educators do not seem to be diminishing anytime soon. In his 2010 book, *Schools Cannot Do it Alone*, Jamie Vollmer sheds light on the amount of required programs added to educators' responsibilities over the years. As mentioned in Chapter 1, more than thirty-two programs have been added to the plates of public school employees since 1990 and, presumably, even more since the publication of this book. While the demands continue to increase, many of the resources have remained static. The length of the instructional day has not changed in over sixty years while public school funding is not at an acceptable level for many districts and can be considered appalling in other areas of the country. The demands of the education profession continue to pile up as teachers and staff are being asked to tackle many of the issues of society without the necessary tools. Needless to say, if we continue along this trajectory in the education profession, burnout is inevitable.

While a dismal picture has been painted in the preceding paragraphs, hope exists in the way of intentional individual and organizational interventions. The needs of educators can be addressed to manage workload, reestablish control, increase autonomy, while cultivating engagement in our schools. When considering this mismatch, it can become overwhelming thinking how to truly impact change. In this chapter, the mismatch will be broken down into four parts with suggestions provided to address each component:

1. Exhaustion

With so much being demanded along with seemingly depleted resources, educators are overwhelmed with exhaustion that cannot be cured with a good night's sleep. Emotional exhaustion or the feeling of fatigue that is developed when emotional energies are drained is a common experience for the 21st century educator. One of the key indicators of exhaustion is waking up in the morning feeling overwhelmed with the idea of facing another day at school (Leiter & Maslach, 2005). You are too tired to take on the demands that come with your job and sleep is just not fixing the issue. Maybe what you are being asked to accomplish as a principal by your superintendent is not feasible, leaving you with piles of work to complete in the evening. As a special education teacher, perhaps you are responding to behavioral concerns all day and cannot get to your regular responsibilities. Instead, you do this at night rather than dedicating time to your family. Or maybe your school is in a hybrid model of instruction and as a secondary English teacher, you are providing a blend of face-to-face and virtual instruction. Not only are you required to teach onsite students, but you must also prepare digital content. You are being asked to do two jobs, but have not been given any more time or compensation to do so. All these examples demonstrate an imbalance of demands and adequate resources to meet those demands, leaving educators emotionally and physically exhausted. When these feelings become chronic, educators find they can no longer give of themselves to students as they once could. What can be done about this? Consider the following:

How Do You View Your Work? While the number of hours worked does matter, the manner in which work is experienced has shown to be a more indicative measure regarding burnout and engagement. For example, when educators have flexibility, choice, voice, and autonomy with their responsibilities, they report higher levels of well-being and engagement. It is more about how the work is experienced than the number of hours invested in the position.

Let's consider something before we go any further. Whether you are a teacher, administrator, paraprofessional, school counselor, custodian, or fulfilling any other responsibility within the education setting, what would you say if you were asked to describe your role in one of three ways: a job, a career, or a calling? Amy Wrzesniewski and colleagues (1997) have spent several years researching how people identify with their work. They have classified three categories of work: job, career, and calling. Those who identify with a job, see work as a means to a financial end, a way to make money to do the things they want to do when they are away from work. In contrast, those with a career work for the rewards that come from advancement through the organization while moving up the ladder of promotion. People with a career are focused on bettering themselves; increased pay, prestige, and status that come with advancement are a significant motivator of their work. Finally, those with a calling seek deep satisfaction and an emotional connection to their work. The work itself is the reward and people who associate with this orientation believe their work makes the world a better place.

Where do you land? I have worked with custodians who saw their work as a calling. These men and women took pride in providing a safe, clean, orderly, and welcoming environment for students, staff, and visitors to the building. They were maximally engaged and viewed their responsibilities of cleaning and sanitizing as setting the stage for kids to learn and grow. I have also worked with district leaders who viewed their role as a job whether they admitted it or not. Even though they were in a position of high influence, these educational leaders viewed their role simply as a way to make money for outside of school activities. Of course, there are other district leaders who see their work as a calling and cannot imagine doing anything more important and custodians who are simply employed to make some money so they can pursue their true passion.

If you are interested in reducing exhaustion within your role and experiencing your work as a calling, try reframing how you see your responsibilities. For example, suppose you are an assistant principal in a middle school and one of your primary responsibilities is managing student discipline. Without the proper mindset, this role can run you down and challenge your patience and emotions to unprecedented levels. Rather than approaching this as drudgery and something you have to do, try reframing this responsibility as an opportunity where you get to connect with students who need positive relationships more than anyone in the school.

Burnout Behavior: "Have To" Instead of "Get To". Language matters. Many times we refer to tasks that we *have* to do, rather than what we *get* to do. For example: "I have to grade these narrative essays." "I have to attend another negotiation meeting." "I have to respond to this upset parent again." A simple reframe can make all the difference. Don't see things as "have to's," see them as "get to's." You *get to* make a positive impact in all that you do.

Or perhaps you are a seventh grade teacher and are required to supervise in the cafeteria each day. This is a relatively chaotic environment that can be stressful. You can view this as a burden or an opportunity to get to know your students on a deeper level outside the classroom environment. There is power in choice and we have the freedom to choose how we view and respond to our work requirements each day. Will you choose to see your work as a job, a career, or a calling? Higher purpose and clarity is the result of better responses to the various events we experience each day. Better responses can reduce exhaustion and produce better outcomes, as we will discover in the next section.

$E + R = O$: I began listening to Tim and Brian Kight on the *Focus 3 Podcast* many years ago and love the clarity, simplicity, and consistency they provide related to achieving excellence. A good portion of their content is dedicated to a simple, yet powerful equation they established: $E + R = O$. The **E** represents *Events* in our lives, the **R** symbolizes our *Responses* to those events, and the **O** embodies the *Outcomes* we achieve. Of the three factors of this equation, there is only one directly within our control: the **R**. Let's examine each factor of the equation a little closer:

Event - Positive, neutral, and negative events are constantly occurring in our lives. For example, the birth of my two sons were gratifying and exciting **Es** in my life. Eating breakfast this morning was insignificant in the grand scheme, but an **E** nonetheless. Losing my mother to a horrific battle with metastatic breast cancer was an incredibly challenging **E** that still impacts me more than four years later. As an educator, you will experience hundreds of events each day in the workplace as well as social and home environments; some are significant and have a considerable effect, while others are miniscule in the overall picture. We cannot control events; they continue to flow in and out of our lives.

Response - Unlike the events that make their way into our lives, we do have direct control over how we choose to respond to events. If we seek to produce better outcomes, we must train ourselves to develop compelling, productive responses. Consider the six factors below that comprise an effective process to develop better responses to the events you experience. You can find additional commentary of this process in *Above the Line* by Urban Meyer and Wayne Coffey (2015). Here is a brief explanation about responding with precision:

a. **Press Pause:** When faced with any situation, stop yourself and ask, "What does this situation require of me right now?" Some answers might be complex and compelling, while others will be quick and concise. It is important to stop and consider what the event requires of you.

b. **Get Your Mind Right:** Positive thoughts lead to positive action. In this step of the response process, you need to get yourself in the proper frame of mind. If you are not in a good headspace, your response will not be high-quality.

c. **Step Up:** In this stage of the response, it is time to answer the question we first asked ourselves when pressing pause: What does this situation require of me? Once we have determined what is required of us, it is time to act. Step up and take the action you need for the outcome you want to produce.

d. **Adjust and Adapt:** Be prepared to adjust and adapt to different events that come your way. Continue to ask yourself: Are the actions I am taking allowing me to obtain my desired outcomes? If the answer to that question is no, be ready to adjust and adapt.

e. **Make a Difference:** The way you respond creates an event for others. This component is about realizing you are part of something bigger than yourself. Your response (good or bad) makes a difference to others.

f. **Build Skill:** As you continue to respond effectively, you continue to get better and build skill.

Outcome - While we can influence outcomes, we do not have direct control over them. As we experience adverse situations, learning to develop better responses will often result in better outcomes. Now that we have a basic understanding of the model, let's see it in action.

Matt's Story: Several years ago, a student athlete by the name of Matt had a terrible accident with a four-wheeler on his farm in the Midwest. He suffered an awful break in his leg and surgery was required to repair the damage. As time passed, Matt experienced many complications with infection and was forced with an unbelievable decision that no person should ever have to make, let alone a fourteen-year-old boy. Due to complications and bouts with severe infection following the accident, Matt needed to have his leg amputated if he wanted the opportunity to pursue his passion for football and farming in the future. When Matt was a freshman in high school, he moved forward with the procedure, which severed his leg just below the right knee, and immediately began rehabbing to get back to his typical life.

By the time his sophomore season rolled around, Matt was equipped with a state-of-the-art prosthetic leg and ready to join his teammates on the gridiron. He was able to have a very successful season starting at middle linebacker and fullback.

Unfortunately, the setbacks did not stop after the amputation, and Matt had to endure another obstacle during his junior year. The sores and infections returned, forcing him to forgo the season. He did not falter for a second; Matt focused on getting healthy to have the chance to play football as a senior. Although he could not play as a junior, he remained active, serving as a manager, attending every practice, and continuing to work on the mental aspects of the game.

As Matt's senior year approached, he worked exceptionally hard in the off-season to get his body ready for competition and began the regular season with two successful games. In the third quarter of week two, however, Matt suffered yet another set-back, injuring his left knee. The coaches did not know the extent of the injury, other than he was seriously hurt and needed assistance getting off the field. By the following week, Matt was practicing with his teammates, fighting through defensive drills while listening to his left knee click and pop with every movement and cut. After consulting with the trainer, he was sent to the hospital where it was determined he had torn the ACL of his left knee and would need surgery to repair it.

The day Matt went down in the second game of the year, the coaches knew in their core that he would never play football again, but refused to fully believe it. When people talked to Matt about the series of incidents, they continued to express their sympathy.

Matt's series of responses in these four years speak to his character. He steadfastly replied, "You do not need to feel sorry for me. It has been harder than Hell and my patience has been tested, but I can tell you there are people who have it a lot worse than I do. There is no way that I would have been able to develop empathy for others if I didn't go through this. I am a better person because of everything and, for that, I'm grateful."

When I consider resilience, I think of Matt and all that he experienced in those four years. He continually went through the wringer, but came out with a smile on his face and an incredible passion to be better each day. I can only hope that our students, teachers, staff, and my own children develop some of the resilience he possesses. If we are in the education field long enough, we will get knocked down more times than we can count. However, we can not only pick ourselves up with improved responses, but also become better *because* of the falls.

Physical Fitness: In addition to better responses through the E + R = O model, ~~physical fitness and exercise can allow a clearer head, reduce physical pain, and build resilience in the face of challenges~~. I define resilience as a combination of a positive mindset and physical well-being. By building resilience you can combat the most definitive element of burnout: exhaustion. Improving your resilience will not shield you from all demands and challenges at school; however, it does improve your ability to respond in the face of adversity. A physical and mental routine such as aerobic exercise, strength training, mindfulness meditation, or yoga may work for you and lay a solid foundation for taking charge of your life at work, while establishing a sense of control. The benefits of exercise on the mind and body will be discussed in further detail in the *Caring for You* section at the end of this chapter.

2. Being Too Available

Contributing to the emotional exhaustion that comes with workload challenges is the inability to say no or making ourselves too available. Consider Marcus at the beginning of the chapter. In addition to his highly demanding role as a high school administrator in an urban setting, he said "Yes" to serving as an adjunct professor at a local university, a youth basketball coach (twice) for his girls, and preparing multiple presentations at a national conference. While Marcus is an achiever by nature, saying yes to all these opportunities made him too available and left him tired, overweight, negative, and questioning his effectiveness.

Burnout Behavior: Saying "Yes" to Everything. Educators are
givers by nature and want to help whenever they can. Directly
and indirectly, it has been signaled to educators in the school context that in order to be effective, they must coach or sponsor an
after school activity, serve on several committees, attend parent/
teacher organization meetings, and organize social events for the
staff. Energetic teachers and administrators tend to say yes to
almost all requests because they want to help push the organization forward. This often occurs early in the career of an educator,
as many of us want to show our commitment, or prove our worth.
Please don't misunderstand me. Being involved in school activities, committees, and so forth are critical for school success. However, without clearly articulated individual core values of what
matters most, it can be difficult (especially for newer educators)
to establish boundaries, which can quickly lead to overextension.
Keep in mind, when you are consistently saying yes to all requests,
you are saying no to something else. Without establishing clear
boundaries and training ourselves to say no with skill, we can easily go down a path similar to Marcus.

In *Dare to Lead* (2018), Brene Brown states, "Setting boundaries is
making clear what's okay and what's not okay, and why" (p. 39). When
you think about workload, control, and autonomy in your position,
are there boundaries that are being violated? For example, do you find
yourself sending or responding to emails at all hours of the evening? Is
there a boundary that you could establish with others that communicates what's okay and what's not okay, and why? If you are struggling
to accomplish everything during the day and find yourself bringing
work home every night of the week, consider establishing a block of

uninterrupted time once or multiple times per week to tackle your top priorities.

In order to make this work, you will need a block of time and a prioritized list of your key tasks. If you are a teacher, this could be your prep time and if you are an administrator, counselor, instructional coach, or superintendent, perhaps you have more discretionary control of your calendar when students are not directly in front of you. The key is to schedule this time daily or a couple of times per week while establishing and communicating boundaries with your colleagues about how this time will be used. Put this time on your calendar and commit to it. As a principal, having an open door policy is very important to me. However, every Thursday I schedule a block of time with myself and shut my door for an hour to prepare the *Friday Focus* memo for staff. It is important to me that the *Friday Focus* is delivered at the same time each Friday morning so our staff members can rely on it. Before establishing what I refer to as "the hour of power," I found myself writing this Thursday evenings or very early Friday mornings, which took away from my time to be a dad or husband. Now that I have established this practice, I leave school on Thursday evenings with a sense of control, knowing the task is complete. *Para feedback time?*

If you are a teacher, perhaps it is preparing lesson plans for the following week, providing feedback on a recent assessment, or catching up on your email. If you are a superintendent, maybe this uninterrupted time would be used to prepare your weekly school board update or an upcoming presentation to the community. Whatever your role, the key to this practice is setting the time on your calendar, not allowing anyone to impede on it, and being extremely clear with yourself about what you will accomplish. You will be amazed at what you can get done with just twenty-five minutes of uninterrupted, focused time.

A high school principal that I know in the Midwest uses a variation of this practice weekly. Every Sunday evening around 6:00, he travels ten miles to a coffee shop to complete a variety of tasks aimed at getting organized for the upcoming week. He puts in his earbuds and gets to work, responding to emails from the previous week, previewing all the upcoming events at his high school, and preparing a *Monday Memo* to keep his staff in the communication loop. Once these tasks are finished (which is usually around 8:00 or 9:00 p.m.), he heads home with a clear head and a strong sense of control about the upcoming week. His reason for going to a coffee shop ten miles away from his home is an intentional step to limit distractions.

I have seen other educators use this block of time as a modified version of the "Shultz Hour." George Shultz was secretary of state in the 1980's and liked to carve an hour out of his incredibly busy schedule each week for quiet reflection. It has been said that he sat down in his office with a pad of paper and a pen, closed the door, and told his secretary the only people allowed to interrupt him were the president and his wife. I have seen principals and superintendents across the country utilize this technique in their work routines to intentionally focus on the important, bigger picture items on their lists.

3. Not Enough Time

A couple of times per week, as I scroll through my Facebook and Twitter feeds, I find at least one blog post or article dedicated to productivity tips, strategies, or apps to help educators make the most of their time, while balancing their workloads. The next new tool or quick-fix strategy is often highlighted as a way to solve the workload issues educators continue to experience. Ironically, the smartphones in our pockets loaded with time management and productivity apps designed to help us become more efficient are inadvertently contributing to the problem. Without proper boundaries, educators are continually overwhelmed with emails, text messages, and other notifications at all hours.

Burnout Behavior: Email at All Hours. If you so desired, I am convinced that you could check email twelve hours a day and still have messages sitting in your inbox. The more we send, the more we get. If you are a school leader, keep in mind that what you model is what you get. If you send a ton of emails, expect to get a ton in return. Additionally, if you send emails after hours, expect to receive emails after school hours. Sending email after hours communicates to those you serve that they should do the same thing. Email can lead to overextension if we are not conscious about our habits.

On the one hand, my iPhone is a lifeline and there are many applications that make my life easier. However, addressing workload, control, autonomy, and the issue of time is more about human behavior than tools, tricks, or hacks.

Before we dig too far into providing solutions to these issues, we need to establish some clarity. While items continue to get added to our plates and to-do lists, we need to be reminded that we are all working from the same set of restrictions related to time. As much as we may want more of it, there are only 24 hours in a day, 168 hours in a week, 52 weeks and 365 days in a year. This means we are all working with the same amount of time day in and day out. However, we can control how we choose to use our time. Like former Disney executive Lee Cockerell (2015) says, "Most people are not overworked... they are under-organized" (p. 20).

We have choice, voice, and autonomy when it comes to work completion, prioritization, and efficiency. Will you spend your time responding to emails in your office at all hours of the day or building the capacity of those around you? Will you watch the hours pass by while completing compliance reports or will you lead those within your charge to higher levels?

Former United States President, Dwight Eisenhower was considered a master of productivity and is said to have claimed the most urgent decisions are rarely the most important ones. Important activities have an outcome that leads us toward the achievement of our personal and professional goals. Meanwhile, urgent activities demand immediate attention, and are usually associated with achieving someone else's goals. Urgent tasks are often the ones we concentrate on and demand attention because the consequences of not dealing with them are immediate. Without an intentional daily plan, school leaders can be consumed by continually responding to the many urgent fires that come their way.

As we have established throughout this chapter, there are simply too many demands to meet with our current resources, which is why it is critical to establish daily priorities within a to-do list. Employing Eisenhower's Urgent/Important Principle allows you to think about priorities, and determine which of your activities are important and which are distractions. Begin by brainstorming all the tasks you need to accomplish on a list. This can be on a paper list within a planner or electronically, whatever works for you. From this list, you will need to establish priorities that land at the top. When making decisions related to priorities, it is critical to place the urgent and important categories at the top of your list; these are the items that should be completed first. Next will be the important, but not urgent, items, followed by not important, but urgent, and, finally, not important and not urgent tasks. My advice when considering the final two categories (not important/urgent and not important/not urgent) is to delegate these tasks or ignore them altogether. Let's take a closer look at each of the four quadrants:

Urgent and Important: Urgent tasks are sensitive to time, possibly because they have been ignored until they can no longer wait. These tasks can be anything from responding to emails and returning phone

37

calls, to realizing that you have a report due in twenty minutes. When we're not proactive and systematic with important tasks, we're setting ourselves up to make poor decisions. The urgent and important tasks should be our first priority of the day. When I am making my daily to-do list, these tasks are tagged with an asterisk followed by a number (*1, *2...) to indicate which to tackle first.

~~Important but Not Urgent: Important but not urgent tasks are calculated and deliberate.~~ They are ~~bigger picture items we want to accomplish, such as designing a new professional learning structure or researching a method for sharing your school's story on multiple digital platforms.~~ We want to pay attention to these tasks, because they are significant to us. Rather than being reactive and erratic, with the right planning (such a Schultz Hour), we can be thoughtful and engaged with the work we truly want to do. Being proactive with important tasks will maximize your chances of keeping on track and help you avoid the stress of your workload becoming more urgent than necessary. I label these "Important" items on my to do list as $I_1, I_2...$ to make sure I do not forget about them. Additional examples of these tasks could include:

+ Developing the master schedule with embedded collaboration time for teachers for the following school year.
+ Considering a completely different approach to writer's workshop in your classroom.
+ Leading individual conversations with certified and non-certified staff members.
+ Completing classroom walkthroughs and providing appropriate feedback to teachers.

When thinking about your bigger picture, complex items on your to-do list, consider the practice of condensing larger tasks into small, manageable steps to create success. Shawn Achor (2010) refers to this as the "Zorro Circle Principle." Our brains need to experience quick wins to create and sustain lasting change. When larger tasks are broken down, a message is sent to our brains that our behavior matters, and our locus of control is improved. Individuals with a strong internal locus of control believe events in their lives come primarily from their own actions and behaviors. For example, people with a strong internal locus of control credit successes and challenges to their skills and behavioral patterns. Conversely, those with a strong external locus of control tend to praise or blame external factors for what happens, such as other people or the circumstances they are currently experiencing. Breaking tasks down allows us to regain control by focusing first on small, manageable goals and then gradually expanding to achieve larger ones. This is particularly useful when tackling our important but not urgent tasks to keep us on track to doing the work that truly matters.

Not Important but Urgent: These are tasks that prevent you from achieving your goals and vision. When these things make it to your desk, ask yourself whether you can reschedule, delegate, or throw them out completely. Other people are often the source of not important but urgent tasks. It is appropriate to say no to these items respectfully, encourage people to solve the issue themselves, or delegate the task to someone who can assist.

Delegation may have a negative connotation for a variety of reasons. Maybe you had a supervisor in the past who delegated everything and you do not want to repeat this approach. Or perhaps you have concerns about the follow-through or quality of the delegated tasks. Both of these concerns are legitimate; however, looking at delegation through a different lens can make all the difference. Rather than thinking about giving work away through delegation, consider this as a capacity building and leadership opportunity for your team. Is there someone on your staff who could complete the task which would increase their capacity and allow them to grow? When I consider delegation in this light, there are all kinds of urgent but not important tasks that could be given to someone on my team. For example, early in my career as a principal, I would take responsibility for planning all our celebration assemblies. I enjoyed this work at first, but as more demands came my way, this task was put on the back burner and, as a result, often became urgent problems. I thought I was doing our staff members a favor by taking on this responsibility, but ultimately, I was robbing someone else of doing something about which they were passionate. There are countless examples of similar situations that not only wore me down, but took valuable leadership opportunities away from fellow team members. The key to delegation is thinking about it in terms of building the leadership and capacity of others. This not only allows you to lead, but also frees you to do more work of significance.

Not Important and Not Urgent: These items and activities are simply a distraction and should be avoided or deleted from your list altogether. Keep in mind, other people might be counting on you to complete them, even though they do not contribute to your desired results. Say no with skill (using tools such as those listed in this chapter's *Engagement Enhancers*) to these items and provide context of why you cannot do them. If you are consistently clear with your boundaries around unimportant and non-urgent tasks, people will often avoid asking you to complete these tasks in the future.

4. Micromanagement

Micromanagement is a controlling leadership style that can rear its ugly head if we're not intentional about our approaches. As educational leaders, it is natural and necessary to set the vision and direction of the organization, while establishing procedures, routines, and expectations. However, it can become demoralizing and counter-productive, when the desire for control to make sure every detail or every task goes according to plan results in lesser autonomy and empowerment of those we lead. This only creates more problems in the long-term. When you micromanage, you're communicating to those you serve and lead that you don't trust them enough to work on their own and still produce strong results. When educators constantly feel as if everything they do is scrutinized, they become frustrated and stressed out at work–which often leads to exhaustion and, ultimately, burnout. Not only that, but they will feel a loss of autonomy, which can impact their work performance and capacity to be creative, solve problems, and excel in their roles. In other words, micromanaging employees doesn't just breed resentment, it makes them dependent on further micromanagement to do their jobs.

In the 1960's, Douglas McGregor hypothesized that leaders subscribe to one of two theories when attempting to motivate their employees (McGregor, 1960). *Theory X* states that people work because you pay them, and if you don't monitor their every move, they will stop working or do a poor job. *Theory Y* holds that people work for intrinsic motives, that they work harder and better when not being ordered around, and that they do it for the satisfaction they receive from quality

> Employees typically become the kind of worker their leader expects them to be.

work (Achor, 2010). It turns out that leaders who subscribe to *Theory X* have employees who need constant supervision, while those who believe in *Theory Y* have workers doing their jobs for the love and fulfilment of their responsibilities. Employees typically become the kind of worker their leader expects them to be. In my view, leaders must be willing to give their people a certain degree of autonomy and decision-making authority if they hope to refrain from living in a *Theory X* world.

41

An effective leader provides strategy, goals, boundaries, and expectations and then lets the team set the path to meet those expectations. Successful leaders share the "why" first, then empower the people to achieve the "how" and "what."

Tips to prevent micromanagement: Create a more autonomous environment by following these suggestions:

+ Offer choice and voice in a variety of learning opportunities. When all educators have the chance to learn new skills of their choice, they can offer more input into your school's initiatives and professional learning plans.
+ Create an environment in which educators of all levels have a chance to take on more responsibilities. When leadership is more evenly distributed throughout the workplace, you can prevent one person from having excessive control or taking on too much. This is often done in committees, professional learning communities, and other groups in schools. Do not underestimate the positive impact of these teams.
+ Trust your people. As long as team members are hitting their targets, you can trust that they are being productive. After you have explained the "why," trust your people to solve the "what" and the "how" with appropriate guidance.
+ Create clarity. A more laid back work environment can help educators learn to be responsible on their own. Make your school and district policies, practices, and procedures clear, brief, and sensible.

The Path Forward

Amid all the stress and challenges related to workload, control, and autonomy, our brains chart different paths to help us cope. Shawn Achor

(2010) writes about three mental tracks the brain follows when experiencing hardship. After a calamity or misfortune, the first path directs you to stay where you are; you are no better or worse after experiencing the challenging event. The second path leads toward a dark road. Not only do we experience the negative event, but what follows are additional negative consequences. In severe cases, this has been referred to as post-traumatic stress disorder. The third and not-so-common route is the road toward resilience. Resilience is about navigating the course that not only leads out of failure or suffering but allows us to be more fulfilled and successful; adversity is actually used to one's advantage to find the way forward. Research has shown that when people are able to reframe stress and adversity not merely as challenges, but as opportunities, they are more likely to experience growth. Tedeschi and Calhoun (1995) identified the positive psychological changes that can occur following a potentially traumatic event as *Post-Traumatic Growth*. The five components of Post-Traumatic growth identified by these researchers are: improved relationships with others, openness to new possibilities, greater appreciation of life, enhanced personal strength, and spiritual development.

Consider Matt Riniker, the young man discussed earlier in the chapter who faced enormous adversity. During the four years of his high school career, he was repeatedly faced with setbacks, but refused to see these events as threats; rather, he viewed them as opportunities to get better. In fact, he mentioned his gratitude for all he endured because he developed higher levels of empathy and understanding for others. This is the essence of choosing the third path: not just getting through the adverse event but coming out of it better than when you arrived. Educators can place themselves in a position to respond effectively in challenging times to tackle their workload dilemmas. There will be no shortage of unfavorable situations and by crafting quality responses aligned to personal values, our chances to act effectively increase dramatically.

1. **Protect Your Schedule** - Without careful discipline, it becomes easy to overextend your daily schedule. It is important to realize and remember that not all tasks are created equal. When planning your day, make sure that you schedule and protect precious time. For example, if exercise, meditation, reading, creative projects, or uninterrupted time to think and strategize are important to you, make sure it is on your calendar and do not make other commitments during these blocks of time. If you have children and a spouse at home, I assume that spending quality time with them is important. It may sound hokey, but schedule this as well. We are not obligated to be available at all times. In addition to your required tasks, make sure to carve out pockets of non-negotiable time for what's important to you. An hour of time is the equivalent to 4% of the day. The more intentional and disciplined we are with our schedule, the more likely we will complete tasks that matter, which will cultivate our personal engagement.

2. **Say No with Skill** - When we learn how to say no to things that do not serve us well, we can say yes to the things that do. If we continue to say yes to requests that do not get us closer to our goals or purpose, we continue to function in a reactive state, leading to exhaustion and potentially resentment. Saying no with skill takes disciplined practice; here are a few tips:

   a. Decide what you can say no to. There are certain items that are non-negotiable that you must do. Before you begin this process determine whether you can say no.

    b. When a request comes your way and you have the ability to say no, ask yourself if it adds value, if it will make you happy, or if it aligns with your values. If the answer to any of those questions is no, say no to the request.

    c. Be clear and be kind. When you say no, you don't need to give too much of an explanation. When you do, others can see this as an opportunity to negotiate a yes. My favorite responses are, "No, I'm sorry, I have a commitment." "I'm sorry, this request doesn't fit my direction right now. Please keep me in mind in the future."

3. **Start Meetings with a Win** - This tactic is incredibly simple, but equally powerful. Start each staff meeting, collaborative session, or individual conversation with a win, celebration, or something to look forward to. This can be personal or professional. The key to this tactic is spending a few intentional minutes to connect with one another, while moving people to a positive emotional state prior to tackling the content of the meeting.

4. **Communication Protocol** - With unlimited access through mobile technology, we are more accessible than ever. To combat this issue, I have established what I refer to as a communication protocol with staff members. At the beginning of each school year, I lay out the following plan with our people: If a response is needed within twenty-four hours, they are instructed to send an email. If an answer is needed within an hour, staff members can send a text message or a Voxer (a free phone app we use for communication purposes at our school) message. If I am needed immediately, team members must call my cell phone. Our staff members have respected this protocol, which helps me to be more present in the moment, even away from school. This plan is also helpful to our staff, as they are aware of what to expect and provided with direction in ways to communicate

in the most efficient manner. There are times when a teacher may need assistance from me in responding to a frustrated parent in the evening or when working on another task. When situations like these arise, I ask teachers to send me a text or give me a call, prompting me to check my email to assist.

CARING for YOU

1. **Exercise, Hydration, and Nutrition** - Daily physical activity is a catalyst for happiness and an antidote to exhaustion. It improves mood, releases endorphins, increases energy, enhances sleep, lowers chances of obesity and chronic disease, tends to be a pro-social activity, and is likely to make you feel more attractive (Buettner, 2017). Exercise is not just a powerful mood lifter but also a long lasting one. Run, walk, ride, dance, stretch, skip; it does not matter as long as you get moving. If it gets the heart pumping, it increases energy, gets more oxygen to the brain, and increases endorphins, which will boost your mood and performance. Ratey and Hagerman (2013) found that regular physical exercise provides your brain with just as many benefits as the rest of your body.

   In addition to physical exercise, for your body to function properly, while improving sleep quality, cognitive abilities, mood, energy levels, and overall performance, it is essential to stay hydrated. General guidance on the amount of water to consume each day varies; however, most guidance suggests 64 ounces to half your body weight in ounces is adequate daily intake. If you find difficulty meeting your water consumption goals throughout the day, consider setting targets. For example, if you set out to drink one hundred ounces of water per day, consume thirty-three by 11:00 AM, sixty-five by 3:00 PM, and one hundred by 7:00 PM. It may also help to have an appealing bottle that is easily accessible throughout the day.

The best fuel for your body is healthy food. Healthy foods such as fresh fruits, vegetables, and lean proteins reduce the risk of some diseases, reduce high blood pressure, improve our ability to fight off illness, and increase energy levels. Although it is challenging to establish set mealtimes with a mixture of healthy foods in the fast-paced environment in which educators live, I cannot overemphasize the importance of consuming high-quality food that is filled with nutrients.

2. **Sleep** - It does not matter if you are a teacher, an administrator, or paraprofessional; if you are working in education, your days are busy, filled with emotion, and never short on challenges. Our brains are active during the day and continue to be in school mode even when we are away from the job. The brains and bodies of educators need time to rest, relax, and recharge. Many educators do not get enough sleep, which can adversely impact mood, energy levels, brain function, and stress levels. Furthermore, lack of sleep negatively affects attention, executive function, working memory, quantitative skills, logical reasoning ability, general math knowledge, and even motor dexterity (Medina, 2014). There does not seem to be a magic number regarding the ideal hours of sleep each night, but most guidance suggests seven to eight hours per night is best for most people. A regular routine at bedtime can help, as well as avoiding bigger meals and/or caffeine too close to the time of sleep. Consider powering down your electronic devices at least thirty minutes before bedtime, as the blue light produced by devices can be troublesome to a good night's sleep.

CHAPTER 3

⟋⟍

Practicing Encouragement, Recognition, and Appreciation

"Appreciation can make a day, even change a life. Your willingness to put it into words is all that is necessary."
Margaret Cousins

aylor is in her fifth year as a second-grade teacher at Wilson Elementary School. She entered this position loving everything about teaching. Preparing engaging lessons, delivering content, inspiring her students to think, connecting with colleagues in team meetings, serving on building committees, and participating in professional learning opportunities energizes her. Unfortunately, Taylor is surrounded by negative colleagues who openly criticize students, regularly blame parents and families for the issues they experience with kids, and make numerous passive-aggressive comments behind Taylor's back, mocking her positivity. Professional jealousy is wired into the culture of Wilson School and Taylor is often the victim.

Burnout Behavior: Social Comparison. Social comparisons can be characterized as either upward or downward. When social comparisons are upward, we compare ourselves to someone we believe to be performing better than we are. In contrast, when we engage in downward social comparison, we compare ourselves to someone we believe is not performing as well as us. For the purpose of this burnout behavior, the focus is directed to comparisons that produce negative effects and emotions where you base your personal worth on how you stack up against others. Some examples include: "Taylor is so positive and happy; I'll never be able to be like her." "Michael's family is beautiful and just perfect, why can't we be like that?" "Caryn is so organized and has everything together; if only I could be more like her." There is nothing wrong with aspiring to be better; however, constantly comparing yourself or your situation to others often results in negative emotions including envy, guilt, jealousy, regret, and defensiveness. In the long run, too much comparison is a bad thing.

Although Taylor's principal, Ms. Molina appears to be effective, she has not made any progress addressing the damaging behaviors of some educators at Wilson, nor has she invested the time to recognize Taylor's unique contributions. Ms. Molina spends her days responding to student behavioral concerns, addressing urgent staff needs, and acting on requests from the central office. She is not comfortable with the way that many educators are acting in this school. She tells herself that the negative behavior will be addressed and things will get better when she is able to catch up with some of these urgent demands.

The following week, Ms. Molina is leading a professional learning exercise with the staff at Wilson. Two boisterous teachers continually talk while Ms. Molina is speaking to the entire staff about creating a culture in which students and staff can thrive. These two teachers continue to make faces and roll their eyes when Ms. Molina discusses meeting students where they are. Ms. Molina notices these actions but does nothing to address the behavior. She moves forward with the agenda as if nothing is happening. This has become the norm during professional learning sessions at Wilson. Taylor sees all this and continues to wonder why Ms. Molina is not doing anything about these teachers. Taylor leaves the meeting distraught, feeling horrible for Ms. Molina. The principal has officially ceded her leadership credibility.

Toward the end of the school year, there is an opening at Lincoln Elementary, another school in the district. Taylor likes Ms. Molina as a person, but her principal makes her feel anonymous. Ms. Molina invests her time responding to the demands of the toxic teachers in the school, while neglecting teachers like Taylor. Though extremely difficult, Taylor decides she cannot continue to work at Wilson, requests a transfer, and is approved to teach fifth grade at Lincoln the following year. Taylor initially feels guilty for leaving Wilson; however, she knows her values are misaligned with the school culture and Principal Molina's leadership behaviors. Consequently, Ms. Molina has lost her best teacher and cynicism continues to flourish in this school.

Ms. Molina is interested in creating a culture at Wilson in which students and staff members can thrive and achieve their highest potential. Unfortunately, her responses do not align with this anticipated outcome. Beliefs are not enough; if we are interested in improvement, our behaviors must line up with our beliefs. Ms. Molina was faced with several challenging events and her responses were not strong enough to address the issues, leaving her with undesirable outcomes, including losing her best teacher. When we get it right, by

> Beliefs are not enough; if we are interested in improvement, our behaviors must line up with our beliefs.

focusing on outcomes and responding with encouragement, recognition, and appreciation, great things can happen. While adversity is certain at times in any school setting, it does not mean we have to accept such circumstances without doing all we can to change them.

The Mismatch

According to research conducted by the United States Department of Labor (2002), 64% of Americans leave their jobs because they do not feel appreciated. Seriously, nearly two-thirds of workers depart because they do not feel like their work matters. They are not leaving because of insufficient pay, or because they don't have a ping pong table in the breakroom, or fancy exercise equipment; no, they are departing because they do not feel valued by their organizations. What makes this statistic tragic is the amount of encouragement, recognition, and appreciation (ERA) leaders provide to individuals on their teams is directly within their control and free of charge. According to a 2020 analysis from Gallup, only one in three workers in the United States strongly agree that they received recognition or praise for doing good work in the past seven days. At any given organization, it's not uncommon for employees to feel that their best efforts are routinely ignored. This element of engagement and performance might be one of the greatest missed opportunities for school leaders.

Everyone has the ability to make a difference in the school setting, regardless of their position. It does not matter if you are a paraprofessional, teacher, secretary, principal, custodian, school counselor, cook, instructional coach, or superintendent. We all want to know that what we are doing matters and is making a difference. Personal, relevant, and authentic appreciation leads to higher levels of educator engagement, which means less turnover and absenteeism, increased productivity, and—ultimately—improved outcomes for students. In fact, a

Glassdoor (2013) survey found that 81% of employees are motivated to work harder when their supervisor showed appreciation for their work. It makes sense. When we understand expectations and we are encouraged, recognized, and appreciated for meeting those expectations, we are motivated to do more, feeling that we are making a significant contribution.

Throughout this book, you will hear my argument loud and clear that high-quality people are the most important resource in a school or district. Nothing is more critical to the improvement of a school system than high-quality teachers and staff. Retaining those high-quality educators must be a top-priority for all school leaders.

In their book, *The Five Languages of Appreciation in the Workplace*, Chapman and White (2019) identified five languages of appreciation that motivate people to do their best work. Not all people respond to ERA in the same manner. Different forms are more impactful than others. The five languages are *Words of Affirmation, Quality Time, Acts of Service, Tangible Gifts,* and *Physical Touch.* As we work through this chapter, examples from each language will be embedded within the content.

When You See Something, Say Something

We have all worked with students in various educational settings and when it comes to bullying prevention and school safety, common guidance often goes as follows: *When you see something, say something.* Clearly, this is sound advice and through my experiences, it applies to more than just problematic situations involving students. I came across something similar many years ago when I first started working at a sandwich shop as a college student. I was fortunate to work with fantastic managers who invested in me and provided excellent direction. I vividly remember my first day taking a tour of the shop at the beginning of the fall semester. As I learned about the intricate details of a New Jersey style submarine sandwich, the owner, Bob, shared an important piece of information that has stuck with me to this day. He said, "Dan, in this organization, if the employees are doing something wrong, we're going to tell them. If they are doing something right, we are going to tell them. We will always talk about performance and when we do, we will be as specific and timely as possible." I loved Bob's clear, concise, and direct approach with me. As a young employee, I needed this and took his advice to heart and continued to benefit from this advice when I began serving as a classroom teacher working with my third and fifth grade students. I also used this information as a parent raising my two boys, and finally as a building leader working with many colleagues. Each of these groups crave feedback and work incredibly hard to meet clear expectations. I have shared with them exactly what Bob had told me many years earlier: if you are doing something wrong, I will tell you and if you're doing something right, I'll tell you. This statement is basic common sense; however, the problem is that many people focus only on the first part of the statement.

We See What We Look For

Many years ago, I bought a black Jeep Cherokee and something amazing happened. Every time I was driving, it seemed like I saw a black Jeep on the road. I suspect you can relate to this scenario, because we tend to see what we look for. This is great when we direct our attention to positive behaviors and strengths because we tend to see more of these things. However, when our brains get stuck in patterns that focus on stress, negativity, and problems, failure is inevitable. If one sees the world through the same cognitive patterns for long enough, their brains can retain the imprint of those patterns and fall into what is known as a positive or negative Tetris Effect (Stickgold et al., 2000).

Burnout Behavior: Negativity Bias. You have likely been around someone who simply cannot seem to find the bright side of a situation. This type of person tends to see the negative within all issues. When a child comes home with a report card of four A's and a C, you know what is going to get the attention. When I was a senior in high school, I had the baseball game of my life about midway through the season. In this game, I hit two homeruns, a double, and drove in six runs. I've played hundreds of baseball games in my life and I think I may have hit four total home runs, so this was a special day. After the game, my brother asked what was wrong with me. He pointed out that I struck out and was caught stealing. While this information was accurate, his mind went directly to the negative aspects of the game, rather than my career-best performance at the plate. It turns out, our brains are wired to spot threats and without intentional practice, it can be challenging to find the positive aspects of situations. Identifying mistakes and problems is important and necessary for educators; however, when this becomes the primary focus while neglecting the positives, it is detrimental to our work, relationships, health, and happiness.

A positive or negative cognitive afterimage occurs when people devote focused time and attention to an activity to the extent that it begins to pattern their thoughts, mental images, and dreams (Stickgold et al. 2000). These researchers studied the results from a group of participants who played the computer game, *Tetris*, repeatedly over the course of several days to coin what became known as the "Tetris Effect." Participants were constantly seeing patterns from the game in various settings outside of the laboratory throughout the day. It is crucial to create a positive lens through which to see the world so one can see more aspects of an improved reality. A positive Tetris Effect requires the brain to be actively scanning, scouring, and searching to find a positive pattern (Achor, 2010). When consciously looking for the positive, it becomes easier to find examples of ERA in our schools.

Consider the following questions: When was the last time you felt genuinely appreciated or were provided with encouraging feedback for the work you do? Last week? Yesterday? A few months ago? Maybe you are like Maria from the first chapter or Taylor from this chapter and cannot remember the last time you were recognized or acknowledged at school. If you are in a supervisory role, when was the last time you showed authentic appreciation to one of your constituents? Do we really need encouragement, recognition, and appreciation in our jobs? Isn't that kind of soft? I mean, we get paid for doing our jobs; isn't that enough? Obviously, we work to receive an appropriate amount of compensation to provide for our families and live a full life. My view regarding compensation is in line with what Pink (2009) has written about in *Drive: The Surprising Truth About What Motivates Us*. People should be paid an adequate amount of compensation for the work they do and then it becomes a non-issue. Are we always going to want more money? Probably, but the focus of this argument is not related to financial compensation; it is more about increasing the ERA for those around us, which research has shown makes a difference in performance. ERA is most effective when it is tied to specific positive behaviors, and especially those that reflect organizational values. Educators are more likely to repeat actions for which they're recognized, so consistently sharing ERA is one of the most effective ways to shape your culture. You can create a culture of ERA in your organization by applying the following strategies. They will show you how to foster an environment in which your team is motivated, engaged, and all-in on the mission of your school or district.

Know Your People

At the time of this writing, I have served as principal at my current school for nearly a decade, so I feel like I know our staff members well; however, there is always more to learn to better serve them. It has been and is very important to me to learn about the past experiences of our staff members, as well as their aspirations, preferences, and goals. Over the past few years, I have created a simple interest inventory with Google Forms to send to our staff before the beginning of each school year. The purpose is to get a better idea of their interests, strengths, ways they feel appreciation, names of their family members, what is most important to them in their positions, and so forth. This very simple tactic has proven to be extremely beneficial in terms of not only showing genuine appreciation to our team, but also enhancing relationships. Here are some of the questions I have used on this form to get to know our staff members better:

+ Name of your spouse or significant other (if applicable):
+ Name(s) and age(s) of your children (if applicable):
+ What makes our school unique?
+ As you think about the approaching school year, what do you believe should be our top priority?
+ What is a favorite hot beverage?
+ What is a favorite cold beverage?
+ What is a favorite sweet or savory snack?
+ If you were to go out to eat within the county, where are you heading?
+ If lunch were to be catered to our school, what are you picking?
+ What is your "One Word" for the school year?
+ What is something unique about you that many at our school might not know?

Having this information before the school year begins is beneficial when planning different ways to encourage, recognize, and appreciate staff members throughout the year, as well as developing further connections through authentic relationships. When ERA is personalized and meaningful, the impact is that much stronger and the information provided from this form allows that to happen. Please note a word of caution regarding the staff inventory form: If you are going to spend time creating this and asking your colleagues to spend time completing it, make sure to follow up on the feedback received. Otherwise, this could have an opposite effect when people realize you do nothing with the requested information.

Let Your People Know You

In addition to knowing the strengths, interests, and preferences of those with whom you serve, it is critical for them to get to know you. It is my firm belief that you will get more respect and will be much more successful when you are vulnerable enough to let people know who you really are. I am not suggesting that you share your deepest and darkest secrets with your colleagues, but I am saying that you must clearly communicate your non-negotiables while modeling what you stand for and what you believe in.

Additionally, when others get to know what you value and how you show appreciation, you will be in a much better position to share effective forms of ERA. For example, I know of several principals across the country who organize themes around a variety of appreciation opportunities, complete with matching color schemes, decorations, and the like. Their appreciation celebrations make even the savviest Pinterest users envious. There is nothing wrong with this approach and I'm certain it generates positivity and excitement within their schools; however, this is not my style in terms of ERA. My advice is to get to know yourself, find what works for you, while not trying to be someone else when you are organizing and planning your ERA efforts. As long as your ERA is heartfelt, specific, genuine, and frequent, you will be contributing to an engaging environment.

Social Investment

Happiness research has uncovered the leading indicator for well-being is the strength of our connections with others (Lyubomirsky, 2008). Strong relationships and having social support provide more happiness than income, possessions, IQ, age, gender, ethnicity, or any other factor. Time spent building and maintaining relationships is always a good investment for increasing happiness and organizing activities or events inside and outside the school day to bring people together is beneficial. This brief list is not meant to be exhaustive by any stretch of the imagination. Rather, it provides basic ideas to get you thinking about how to bring people together, while building connections within your space:

"We're not just frying turkeys here": About three times each year, I wake up very early to prepare what I refer to as "Butler's World-Famous Egg Casseroles" for our team members. It is a very simple recipe and staff members really enjoy these days. Throughout the year, there are other occasions when our staff members will be fed. One of my favorites is our annual Thanksgiving meal when our instructional coach (Greg) prepares freshly fried turkeys. As we were preparing this meal at our inaugural Thanksgiving event, Greg turned to me and said, "We're not just frying turkeys here, Dan; we are building culture." To reiterate, it is not about the food. It is all about bringing people together to share a meal and signal that I am of service to them and appreciate their work. The food is simply the vehicle to make this happen.

Holiday Gatherings: I love to host the annual staff holiday party at the Butler residence. From my perspective, it provides a family atmosphere where people can relax, connect, and unwind during a challenging time of year. I realize this practice is not for everyone, but this has worked well for my leadership style as a way of bringing people together in a safe space.

Pick Up the Tab: Many times, our staff members will head to a local establishment to enjoy refreshments after a long week. There are times that I will join; however, often I intentionally do not attend to give people time together away from me. If I know in advance that the staff is going to be gathering in an establishment, I will plan to cover their tab before their arrival. This small sign of appreciation is a nice surprise and communicates that gathering together outside of school is very important.

Walk in Their Shoes: I have always struggled with gifts for our staff members during the holiday season. My hope has been to provide them with something meaningful to communicate they are very much appreciated, while not breaking the bank. A few years ago, I came up with something that I found to be effective. I gave each member of our team *The Gift of Time*. I offered each certified and noncertified staff member a certificate that communicated they had an additional hour of time to do as they chose, and their responsibilities would be covered by me. They could choose to arrive an hour later, take an extended lunch, attend a special event of one of their school-aged children in the middle of the day, or get an early start to the weekend. I asked each staff member to give me a week's notice so I could plan my coverage accordingly. Not only was this gift appreciated by our staff members, but it was also enjoyable for me. I had the opportunity to get a glimpse of the various responsibilities of our staff members. I did everything from serving lunch as a food service worker, to cleaning classrooms as the custodian, to answering phones as the secretary, and teaching literacy groups to kindergarten readers. The *Gift of Time* is a great way to increase ERA in your school and it is completely free of charge.

Notes of Encouragement: There is power in the written word and it turns out there is strong scientific evidence to support this claim. A collection of researchers (King, 2001; Otake et al., 2006; Slatcher et al., 2006) have found that committing a kind act, such as writing a handwritten note, allows the release of dopamine, which is strongly associated with pleasure and often referred to as "the helper's high." Not only is performing a kind act, such as writing a handwritten note, good for you, but it also triggers dopamine in the brain of the person who receives the note. I attempt to start each day by writing a note of encouragement, recognition, and appreciation to staff members; my friend and fellow educator, Jeff Zoul, introduced this practice to me. I might write a note to the custodian for an exceptional job of setting up the gymnasium for an event, or to a teacher for winning an award. I may write some words of encouragement to a paraprofessional having a difficult day with a student or write a couple of lines to a secretary for showing so much love and support to visitors. I do not have specific criteria for these notes of recognition, other than to let people know that I can see that what they are doing is making a difference for our school. My handwritten note practice forces me to scan the environment each day, looking for great things and spreading positivity to staff members throughout the building.

To be as effective as possible with this note-writing habit, it is imperative to make sure your words are authentic, specific, heartfelt, and focused on behavior. Some of the language that I like to use when writing notes focused on behavior includes:

I valued…
Thank you for…
I appreciate your ability to…
I am grateful for…

Of course, these are not the only phrases that work, but this short list does give you an idea of the type of encouragement being provided through this exercise. Do I always write one per day? Nope, but it is my plan to send at least five of these per week. As I started writing these notes many years ago, I knew they were having some type of an impact on our staff because as I traveled to various parts of the school, I noticed teachers and staff had saved them on their desks or work areas.

> **Burnout Behavior: Relying on too much ERA from others.** There is no question that encouragement, recognition, and appreciation are critical if we are going to perform at high levels in the workplace. I have outlined several statistics and a host of benefits associated with ERA. A problem can occur when we rely too heavily on ERA from others to boost our self-worth. While important, relying too much on ERA from others can impede engagement and promote burnout.

Friday Focus

I have been using the *Friday Focus* as a weekly staff newsletter for ten years and originally learned of it from the book, *Motivating & Inspiring Teachers: The Educational Leader's Guide for Building Staff Morale* (Whitaker, Whitaker, and Lumpa, 2009). The *Friday Focus* serves as a typical weekly newsletter for staff members, providing information for everyone in the school, including a listing of upcoming events. However, there are a couple of other important components that enhance the memo, solidifying the message. First, the *Friday Focus* is always extremely positive and supportive. It is intended to elevate staff members and motivate them to continue doing the noble work they do each day. It is not a platform to address negative behavior or solve issues. Secondly, I always include a "Professional Development on the Fly" section, which showcases a podcast episode, an article, a link to a resource, or possibly a quote to provoke thought and reflection. The "PD on the Fly" section is intended to spark further action in the classroom. The content shared is intentional and my hope is that it leads to improved practices. Additionally, there is a

"Thought of the Week" section to close the newsletter. In this segment, I share a personal story related to teaching, learning, and leadership. In addition to attempting to share engaging anecdotes that touch the emotions of our people, I also model vulnerability by sharing some of my personal thoughts and experiences, aiming to build trust.

The *Friday Focus* is sent to each staff member as an email at 6:30 on Friday mornings. The timing feature of Microsoft Outlook allows me to set this each week, so it will be delivered at this exact time. By sticking to this disciplined approach, teachers and support staff have come to expect the *Focus* and many look forward to the delivery. I also print a hard copy, placing one in the mailbox of every staff member. This might seem like a waste of paper, but I want to ensure all staff members have access to this document, because it contains critical information about our school and our direction. In addition to sending the *Friday Focus* to all team members at my school, I include all administrators throughout our district, including central office staff, transportation and kitchen managers, and instructional coaches in each building. The purpose of this inclusion is twofold. First, there are times when I provide words of encouragement, recognition, and appreciation to these various groups of people for the support they provide to our school and district. Secondly, I like to lead with transparency, and this is an opportunity for people outside our building to be kept in the communication loop while having the chance to engage in events taking place at our school.

ERA is a Group Project

While ERA is a necessary component for successful school cultures, it does not rest solely on the shoulders of school leaders. When colleagues share ERA with each other, it involves all members of the team in this critical work, while signaling that appreciation does not always need to come from the top. Jim Knight writes about being a "witness to the good" in *High Impact Instruction: A Framework for Great Teaching* (2012) and while this practice is something that aligns with the principles outlined in the book, this evolved from staff members at our school. Once again, a simple Google Form was created and shared with all members of the staff for easy entry at any time. The form has two questions:

1) Please write the first and last name of the person you are recognizing.
2) Starting with the person's name, please share your positive message below.

As with all Google Forms, these answers are populated into a spreadsheet upon submission and I receive a notification when a form has been completed. These digital shout outs are shared with all staff members in the *Friday Focus*, our weekly staff newsletter. The great part about *Witness to the Good* is it allows all staff to participate in encouraging, recognizing, and appreciating their colleagues; the ERA does not always have to come from the principal.

Burnout Behavior: Not Accepting Praise from Others. As we navigate challenging demands in our schools, we are often preoccupied with many tasks and cannot seem to accept the praise or appreciation provided to us. We're too busy thinking about the next thing on our to-do lists or making sense of the many thoughts swirling around in our heads. In the midst of this chaos in our minds, we ignore the wealth of gratitude being sent our way. If it hasn't been modeled for you, accepting gratitude is harder for some than others. When compliments come your way and are dismissed, you not only miss out on an opportunity to boost your mood and engagement, but also make the person delivering the praise feel lousy or awkward. The beauty of responding to gratitude in a meaningful way is that it doesn't shut down a conversation, but rather, opens it up for a more meaningful exchange.

Certainly, there are many more ways to boost ERA in the school setting and the techniques shared in this chapter barely scratch the surface. I am sure there are many practices or ideas you use to increase encouragement, recognition, and appreciation in your schools and districts. I invite you to share these using #Permission2BGreat on your various social media platforms. The key is to bring awareness to the issue and to be intentional about the impact of ERA as a culture-building strategy.

If educators encourage the unique skills their colleagues have to offer, provide the recognition they've earned, and share genuine appreciation to those connected to their schools, they will eventually produce significantly better results for students, staff, and the school community. Simultaneously, they will increase the motivation of everyone involved, including themselves, and create a positive culture that becomes contagious and creates a ripple effect across the organization.

Gratitude - The essence of a gratitude tactic is to capture unique things for which you are grateful on a consistent basis. R. A. Emmons, a prominent researcher and writer about gratitude, defines it as, "A felt sense of wonder, thankfulness, and appreciation for life" (Lyubomirsky, 2008, p. 89). The content of the gratitude could be anything that the participant chooses: from family, to a warm home, or their physical fitness. To reap the benefits of this intervention, participants are instructed to think of unique things each day or week to record and complete this process until a habit is established. It might work better for you to do this on a daily basis, but if that becomes a tedious process, you may want to scale back. If the gratitude practice becomes a chore, you will not receive the intended benefits. People who record things for which they are grateful trigger their brains to cognitively rewire looking for and seeing patterns for which they are grateful. When we feel gratitude, we benefit from a positive memory in our lives and those who are consistently grateful have been found to be relatively happier, more energetic, more hopeful, and report experiencing more positive emotions (Fredrickson, 2009). In addition to the individual benefits of gratitude, when we express it to others, we strengthen our relationship with them (Seligman, 2011).

24 Hours, No Complaints - The goal of this practice is to go twenty-four consecutive hours without a complaint. If you complain, you need to start the clock over until you are able to accomplish this task. There are some exceptions to the rule when considering being complaint-free for a day. If you are addressing a concern or have a solution in mind, it is completely acceptable to make a complaint. As you engage in this process, I'm convinced you will be amazed by two things. First, this will be harder than you think; however, your ability to solve problems will increase if you are committed. Secondly, your eyes will be opened to many more positive aspects when you direct your focus.

Encouragement Box - As an educator for nearly twenty years, I have collected a number of cards, pictures, newspaper clippings, letters, certificates, and other artifacts that have been given to me over the years. Early in my career, I decided to store these items in a portable file folder, which turned out to be very effective. At least twice per year (over the holiday break and sometime in the summer), I organize my office, get rid of unnecessary materials, and so forth. While doing this, I take the time to look through my encouragement box and immediately get a boost of positive energy. Whether it is a thank you card from a parent or staff member, a letter of congratulations for a job well done, or a picture of a student who gave me a run for my money many years earlier, this practice allows me to refocus on why I do this challenging work. I highly recommend you start an encouragement box and go through it periodically, particularly when you are struggling.

Manage Your Activation Energy - While many of the ideas described in this book may seem like common sense, it is well known that common sense is not always common practice. Having knowledge is only the first part of the battle; without action, knowledge is often meaningless. "Managing Activation Energy" is about developing better habits by designing an environment for growth while removing barriers to change. Well-being, success, and productive change are much more likely if a collection of positive habits have been established (Clear, 2018). Negative habits undoubtedly contribute to struggle, making well-being much more challenging. In order to create any type of positive change, such as an exercise regimen, healthy eating, expressing gratitude, or implementing a meditation routine, there is an initial investment of energy that is required to get started; this is called "activation energy" (Csikszentmihalyi, 1997). Research suggests that three to twenty seconds can transform the likelihood of adopting a positive habit or stopping a negative one (Achor, 2010). Often, it is the initial activation energy that ignites or prevents a positive habit. For example, if a person were interested in establishing a morning exercise routine, he or she could do several things to impact the environment to reduce the required activation energy. This could include preparing a specific workout routine the night before and laying exercise clothes right next to the bed. The more convenient an action, the more likely we are to execute the behavior. Heath and Heath (2010) refer to this as tweaking the environment, "Tweaking the environment is about making the right behavior a little bit easier and the wrong behavior a little bit harder" (p. 183). As you begin to focus on improving your well-being through a variety of engagement enhancers, I encourage you to create a path of least resistance toward positive habits. Lower the activation energy for the things you want to accomplish and increase it for the things you want to avoid. As I mentioned earlier, the techniques I have described in the book thus far are not meant to be a blueprint for success. They are merely ideas that have worked for me and which research literature has supported. Given the challenging circumstances of the educational environment, we all need to find what works for us and make a commitment to following through on our plans.

1. Morning Routine - Establishing and successfully executing a morning routine can do a couple of things for you. First of all, you will start the day with success and secondly, you will establish a sense of control of the day ahead. As you establish or think about putting a morning routine into place, consider what works for you and the time it takes to complete each task. My routine takes me sixty minutes from start to finish and includes five components. When I'm at my best, this is what works for me:

    a. *Hydrate.* As soon as I wake up in the morning, I drink sixteen ounces of water to get started on my hydration goal for the day, while taking a moment to allow my brain to wake up.

    b. *Move.* If the weather cooperates, I will run or walk outside for thirty minutes. Otherwise, I will hit the treadmill inside. The physical benefits of exercise are significant and the mental gains are even stronger.

    c. *Eat.* I take about fifteen minutes to prepare and eat breakfast each morning. I usually eat the same thing each day (egg whites and fruit) for ease and efficiency. While I am eating,

I typically spend ten minutes reading something related to leadership.

d. *Reflect.* After reading during breakfast, I participate in some type of reflection with a notebook. This may include summarizing some of my thoughts after reading or expressing things for which I am grateful.

e. *Prepare.* The final component of the routine is to review my schedule for the day to make sure I am ready to go with everything that I have planned, while setting my intentions for the day.

After these five items are completed, I'm ready to hit the shower, get dressed, and attack the day with enthusiasm. The content of the routine is not as important as the structure. I encourage you to find the tasks that are important to you and build a routine around them.

2. Meditation - A host of positive psychologists have written about the benefits of meditation, which has been shown to focus attention. Haidt (2006) wrote about the practice of mindful meditation and its benefits:

"Suppose you read about a pill that you could take once a day to reduce anxiety and increase your contentment. Would you take it? Suppose further that the pill has a great variety of side effects, all of them good: increased self-esteem, empathy, and trust; it even improves memory. Suppose finally that the pill is all natural and costs nothing. Now would you take it? The pill exists. It is meditation." (p. 35)

Spending a few minutes meditating daily provides a host of benefits, including attentional performance and cognitive flexibility. It also increases one's sense of control and decreases psychological symptomatology. Meditation is a core practice of mindfulness and regular practice can permanently rewire the brain to raise levels of happiness, lower stress, and even improve immune function. An incremental approach can allow practitioners to start slow, while setting a small goal of meditating for one minute each day in the first week, and progressively adding time as success is achieved. There are several apps on the market to assist you in this journey (such as the free version of the *Headspace app*).

CHAPTER 4

Building Community and Relationships

"The greatness of a community is most accurately measured by the compassionate actions of its members."
Coretta Scott King

Nearing the end of the school year, Brad started focusing on how he could continue to build the leadership capacity of the instructional coach with whom he was working. As he received communication for an upcoming leadership conference in Washington, D.C., Brad asked his instructional coach if he wanted to submit a proposal to co-present a session focusing on the principal and instructional coach partnership. Brad's instructional coach, Matt, was very much interested, which worked out well, since they would be working together closely the following year. Much to Brad and Matt's excitement, their proposal was accepted, and they would be traveling to D.C. to deliver a presentation entitled, "A Partnership Approach to School Improvement." Matt could not have been more thrilled about the opportunity to attend a national conference and see this part of the country. Shortly thereafter, Matt learned that he would be the father of not just a fourth child, but also a fifth. Matt and his wife, Catherine, were going to have twins, and, around the time of this conference, their family would include five children all under the age of eight.

As the conference drew closer, Matt approached Brad and asked, "What if we drove to D.C. this summer?" Clearly Brad's facial expressions and body language told a story of their own because Matt immediately came back with, "Listen, the Rocky steps are about a two-hour drive from D.C. and you have no idea how much I want to experience that atmosphere in Philly. It's only about fifteen hours in the car and we will have the freedom to stop when we need; it is a much more flexible option."

Let's clarify something before we go any further: this would be a fifteen-hour drive one way. This was a round trip experience, so that would mean thirty hours together in a car. Brad thought about Matt's proposal that evening and decided to make the drive.

As Brad was considering a conveniently smooth two-hour flight versus a pavement-filled, fifteen-hour drive in a district-issued vehicle journeying through six states, he had a moment of clarity. While spending an entire day driving would be cumbersome and, no doubt, exhausting, this decision aligned with a critical ingredient of successful relationships: meeting people where they are. Matt was not a fan of flying and had only flown once in his lifetime (which had not been a great experience). Was driving across the country in a van inconvenient for Brad at the time? Absolutely. Was it what Matt needed at the time? Without question. When we work through relationships with our significant others, including the families we serve, the students we serve, and the colleagues with whom we serve, we realize it's not always about us and, in this particular case, the fifteen-hour drive might be just what the partnership needed to make it even stronger.

Matt and Brad were able to make it to D.C., the Rocky Steps in Philadelphia, and back home in one piece, eight days before the arrival of Matt's precious new children, Lydia and Leah. Although this thirty-hour trek was long and onerous, if faced with the same decision ten times, Brad and Matt would go the same way all ten, without hesitation. During their time, Matt and Brad talked about school leadership, family philosophy, their favorite podcasts, their strengths, weaknesses, and biggest fears. The amount of vulnerability and trust built between the two of them in four days was worth the 2,100 miles traveled. The expedition laid a solid foundation for Brad and Matt to encourage, recognize, and appreciate each other, as well as the staff members they served. As you read this chapter, it is my hope that the power of positive relationships will not only be reinforced, but that you will also walk away with techniques to enhance community-building in your setting.

The Mismatch

Positive relationships can be described as interactions with others that provide a sense of connection and serve as the foundation for well-being. Amid the challenges and stress that are ever present in the educational arena, a strong social support network is the greatest predictor of both performance and happiness (Achor, 2010). The most successful instructors invest in their friends, team members, peers, and family to drive themselves forward.

Burnout Behavior: Neglecting to ask for help. In this book, I have clearly articulated that there are simply not enough resources to meet the demands educators experience within their roles. The work is challenging every single day, even when things are going very well. When educators are faced with tasks that are overwhelming, challenging, or frightening while working through the grind, they may lose sight of their teams, forgetting they have people in their corners willing to support. They may fear rejection or feel they are bothering others and, as a result, neglect to ask for help. When educators try to do everything themselves during hard times, they are destined to experience burnout.

Previous studies have consistently shown that factors such as social support from colleagues and supervisors, performance feedback, skill variety, autonomy, and learning opportunities are positively associated with work engagement (Halbesleben, 2010). The leading authority on positive psychology, Martin Seligman (2011), asserts that other people are the best antidote to the downs of life and the single most reliable up; social connectedness is one of the best long-term predictors of well-being. Essentially, the more social support you have, the happier you are. Conversely, research from Buettner (2017), who has studied the happiest people in the world, found that loneliness has as harmful an effect on well-being as smoking fifteen cigarettes per day and as you age, your risk for high blood pressure, cardiovascular disease, and dementia increases. Strong relationships and social support provide more happiness than income, possessions, IQ, age, gender, ethnicity, or any other factor. Time spent building and maintaining relationships is always a good investment for increasing happiness and promoting engagement. We do not have to look too deeply within the educational literature, Facebook, or LinkedIn posts to see that positive relationships make a significant difference in peoples' lives. Although I will provide additional support of these theories, my main objective is to bring the theories to life by sharing effective practices.

Vulnerability

It is Sunday evening, March 15, 2020, around 8:00 p.m. and I am sitting in my kitchen with my computer and calendar, preparing for the upcoming week. I just finished reading to my youngest son and told my older son goodnight and sent him downstairs to read his book before going to sleep. There was nothing special about this night until my wife received a notification from a local news affiliate on her phone:

"Governor Reynolds recommends all schools in Iowa close for the next four weeks, due to the Coronavirus Pandemic."

What happened over the next three hours could most accurately be described as a s*** storm. My phone started blowing up with calls, text messages, and emails from all kinds of people wondering what in the world was going on and how our district was going to respond. To make matters a little more challenging, my superintendent was out of state, leaving our leadership team to communicate with him from a distance, as well as getting in touch with each other. There wasn't any notice leading up to this announcement by the Governor; we were expecting students to come through our doors in less than eleven hours prior to this communication bomb being dropped.

Over the course of the next three hours, my administrative colleagues and I received more than three hundred text messages (mostly from each other), well over one hundred fifty emails, with about eighty phone calls thrown into the mix as well. With such limited notice, many decisions needed to be made immediately, like who would be reporting to school the next day. Teachers? Custodians? Office staff? What would these four weeks look like for students? Would we be responsible for providing any type of content? These questions were just the tip of the iceberg and they kept coming.

These three hours were memorable to me for two reasons: first, it was intense. My phone vibrated with a new text message at least every thirty seconds for three consecutive hours. In between these vibrations, the notification bell sounded on my Microsoft Surface when a new email arrived. In addition to the sensory overload I was experiencing, I vividly remember the vulnerability demonstrated by our administrative team. Like every educator across the country, we were all taken aback by this announcement and at the beginning of this chaos had no idea what we were going to do. We asked a ton of questions of each other, sought advice, asked more questions, disagreed openly, agreed on several items, and met in the middle on some others. I could not sleep that night because of the adrenaline pumping through my body while worrying about our students and their families. However, it helped to feel good about the exchange of ideas among my fellow leaders and the plans we made for moving forward. Our open communication and ability to expose ourselves for the good of the overall administrative team allowed us to come up with the best answers to the many questions we were receiving.

The following quote from Daniel Coyle (2018) in *The Culture Code: The Secrets of Highly Successful Groups* accurately summarizes the three hours our administrative team experienced after the Governor's announcement: "Vulnerability is about moments that don't feel so beautiful. These moments are clunky, awkward, and full of hard questions. They contain pulses of profound tension as people deal with hard feedback and struggle together to figure out what is going on" (p. 98). We did not know what we were doing, but leaned into the situation, relied on each other, and came out with as solid a plan as possible. Most of you reading this book experienced a very similar communication bomb being dropped in your own districts related to school closures at the beginning of the Coronavirus pandemic. This was certainly a shared vulnerable experience for all educators across the country.

Before I go deeper with my thoughts and experiences regarding vulnerability in the school setting, it is essential to address two important misconceptions. First, vulnerability is not soft, fluffy, or touchy-feely. Vulnerability in the context of team and relationship building is about being OK with personal shortcomings, weaknesses, or misunderstandings. It is about accepting feedback, meeting people where they are, the willingness to ask for help, and having the courage to grow through our failures. Embracing vulnerability is hard and does not happen overnight.

Burnout Behavior: Holding onto resentment. If you are in education long enough, you will undoubtedly experience disappointment. You could be let down by a colleague who says something judgmental, a student who struggles to stay regulated and destroys the classroom out of frustration, family members who criticize your responses to difficult leadership decisions, or your administrator who seems overly critical during an evaluation conversation. The source of the disappointment could be a lack of follow-through, dishonesty, or a failure to live up to expectations. These disappointments may be small, while others significant and full of emotions. Regardless of the size of the letdown, holding onto resentment is not a good thing. Although common, when left unaddressed over a long period of time, resentment can have a negative impact on your well-being, producing feelings of anger, frustration, and a host of other adverse emotions. Valuable time is spent being irritated over something that may not even be on the radar of the other person, which ultimately contributes to burnout.

Secondly, when it comes to optimal team performance and cohesive relationships, vulnerability precedes trust, not the other way around. I have been around many leaders who believe once they establish trust, then they will become vulnerable with the people they serve. If we are interested in establishing high levels of trust within our schools, it is necessary to first become vulnerable

> When it comes to optimal team performance and cohesive relationships, vulnerability precedes trust, not the other way around.

with each other, which will ultimately lead to trusting relationships. Not only is it necessary for leaders to model vulnerability, but it is equally critical to create an environment that encourages vulnerability. How does this happen? Let me take you through a powerful process that required high levels of vulnerability from all members of a team.

Video Learning Teams

I have been coaching football for the better part of twenty years. Something I have always enjoyed as a coach (not so much as a player) is using video to improve performance. When I served as a defensive coordinator, I could not wait to get my hands on the film to identify strengths and the areas where we could grow as a defensive unit. Furthermore, I was equally excited to see our upcoming opponents on video, searching for ways to attack vulnerable spots in their offense. I eventually learned that what worked for me as a football coach might also work in terms of improving the performance of teachers.

About seven years ago, I had the opportunity to attend a three-day workshop with Jim Knight on the University of Kansas campus in Lawrence. Our school district was one of thirty-one districts in the state to receive a Teacher Leadership and Compensation grant that would provide the financial resources to employ nine instructional coaches. Little time was wasted with our newly appointed instructional coach and administrator teams to learn from the leading authority in this area of education. While there were many incredible instructional practices I learned in this workshop, one that stood out was the idea of using video to improve instruction. Video is an essential component of Knight's work and it did not take me long to realize how impactful this could be in terms of school improvement. Following the workshop, we started using video with teachers to drive reflection, track student engagement, and improve instructional delivery. Administrators across our district modeled the practice to create a sense of safety with teachers and we were well on our way. Eventually, we lost sight of the focus and our video efforts fizzled out. It was not until a few years later that my instructional coach and I stumbled across another piece of Knight's work: *Focus on Teaching: Using Video for High Impact Instruction*. In this book, Knight writes about a concept he refers to as Video Learning Teams (VLTs). In a nutshell, teams of teachers get together to watch videos of each other teaching while discussing strengths as well as opportunities for growth. Sounds simple and impactful, right? Remember when I said vulnerability is hard and does not happen overnight? Well, I meant it and VLTs are an excellent example. While this concept is incredibly meaningful and well worth the effort, there is a tremendous amount of psychological safety required to be successful in this process. For principals new to a building, VLTs might not be the best thing to do in your first year, but I want to share my experience with VLTs and the indisputable effect I witnessed it have in our school.

About two years ago, I was not satisfied with our building-level professional learning efforts. To be clear, we were not doing anything wrong. The content provided to educators was relevant. Teachers were engaged in the professional learning process and growing as a result; nevertheless, we were not moving the needle as much as we would have liked. I needed something to not only enhance the instructional skills of our team, but also a structure to bring people together. VLTs became the answer. It was important to create the right teams to provide teachers with the full experience. For example, I did not want all fourth-grade teachers to be on the same team with third grade teachers. Their grade levels and content are too similar. I wanted teachers to examine practices they might not normally observe and have conversations with colleagues they might not see every day. Once the teams were created, we discussed objectives of this process. There were two main goals:

1. Observe and have conversations centered around excellent instruction.
2. Build community with each other.

To fit our professional learning plan for the year, while ensuring each teacher would have the opportunity to serve as a host, we decided to include four members on each team. A typical group at an elementary school might consist of a fourth-grade teacher, a reading specialist, a preschool teacher, and a second-grade teacher. There is no right or wrong way to do this; however, I do believe that having a variety of positions and personalities on each team enhances the experience.

A host from each team was identified for the first round and these teachers were responsible for recording a short (12-18 minutes in length) video of themselves teaching a lesson of their choice to share with their team. The host had absolute control of what they wanted to record. It could be a whole group lesson, small groups, or possibly a one-on-one intervention with a struggling student. The content of the video did not matter; it was all about the feedback the host wanted to receive. The video was recorded in advance and ready to go for the upcoming professional learning day. At the start of the VLT, the host teacher walked the rest of the team through the process, which is as follows:

+ **Pre-Video (5-10 minutes):** This time is used to set up the video. The host explains the main components of the lesson, as well as some context about the students being observed. The host teacher shares their focus and important elements for the team to observe.

+ **During the Video (12-18 minutes):** The group watches the video together and takes notes, paying particular attention to the focus area, questions they have, and additional observations.

+ **Post Observation (30 minutes):** The host teacher facilitates a conversation with the group about their observations, including the focus area and any questions or clarifications that need to be addressed. Sample questions could include:
  + What did you see related to my focus area?
  + What were the students doing?

+ What was I (the teacher) doing?
+ What other observations did you make?
+ If I were to teach this lesson again, what could I change to make it more successful?
+ Are there any questions or items to clarify?
+ **Next Steps (5 minutes):** A few minutes are dedicated for the host teacher and other members of the team to reflect on their learning, while identifying at least one action step. These prompts could include:
  + My biggest takeaway was...
  + With this new learning I will...
  + The support(s) I will need to make this happen include(s)...
+ **Share Next Steps (5 minutes):** The VLT meeting concludes with each person sharing their biggest takeaway from the process.

As you can see, this practice can be wrapped up in about 60-70 minutes, which is time very well spent. As I facilitated VLTs with several teams of teachers, I was incredibly proud of the ideas that were generated to better serve students. I was even more proud of the community that was built among our teachers. We are fortunate to have a close-knit staff who get along with each other well. However, prior to VLTs, I do not remember them regularly talking about instruction with each other. This process allowed time and space for those conversations to occur and the collaboration was not limited to professional learning days. I regularly overheard first grade teachers talking with fourth grade teachers about reading comprehension strategies in the whole group setting. It was not uncommon for me to see a second-grade teacher making the time to connect with a preschool teacher all the way across the building because they had developed a friendship through their VLT.

The success of these groups would have never happened had we not let our guard down to become extremely vulnerable with each other. Vulnerability is the secret sauce of trust. Allow me to reveal a

few more ingredients in that secret
sauce, while explaining another way
to enhance trust in your school.

> **Vulnerability is the secret sauce of trust.**

Keeping the Engine Running

If we think of a school building as an automobile engine, then effective and efficient communication is the oil necessary to power the machine. I apologize in advance to the car experts who are reading this book. I know next to nothing about cars and do not claim to be an expert in the least. In fact, I am somewhat ashamed to admit that even though I am a 41-year-old adult, my father still routinely changes the oil in my vehicle. I know; it is sad. In talking with my father over the years during these oil changes, I have learned just enough to develop a comparison that I think makes sense. For an engine to function effectively, it needs an appropriate amount of clean oil. Without a proper supply of oil, the various components of the engine will not be lubricated, eventually causing friction, debris, and an unavoidable breakdown. It works the same way within schools regarding communication.

Burnout Behavior: Working lunches. Perhaps you are like me and when you hear that there will be a working lunch during a meeting or learning session, you cringe. To be honest, I am someone who enjoys meetings and professional learning opportunities. I am a learner and these gatherings feed a key attribute of mine. However, when it is decided to power through the content and work through lunch, a critical opportunity is missed for the group to relax, recharge, and connect with each other. Working through lunch as the default setting is a recipe for disengagement and potentially a contributing factor of burnout.

Without multiple, consistent methods of open and honest interactions, the countless parts of the school are not going to function at a high level and a breakdown of some sort becomes inevitable. Just as the oil provides lubrication while reducing friction, communication feeds the people inside and outside the organization with relevant information to operate at a higher altitude.

"I wish my principal would not communicate so much. She provides so much clarity about upcoming events, our direction, our school values, and she shows so much appreciation that it gets annoying." I do not believe there is an educator in the United States who would make this statement. It is the leader's job to regularly communicate what is important and what is happening; overcommunication is simply an impossibility. No one leaves a job because of too much communication. With so many moving parts in the educational context, everyone wants to be kept in the communication loop so they can do their jobs as effectively as possible. Leaders have their hands full communicating with various groups in the school setting. Whether they are keeping staff members informed of weekly events through a *Friday Focus* memo (see chapter 3), responding to email questions and requests from teachers and staff, engaging in face-to-face conversations in the hallways, or promoting events to the greater community using a variety of digital tools, communicating effectively with all stakeholders is perhaps the most important responsibility of a leader. Keeping the messaging open and transparent allows everyone in the school settings to be on the same page, while promoting dialogue, addressing misconceptions, building trust and clarity, and ultimately, enhancing relationships.

Individual Conversations

When I first learned that I would be the principal of only one school (previously, I served as principal at two campuses simultaneously), I started thinking about how I could use the additional time I would have on my hands to move the building forward. Whenever I conducted a summative evaluation conference with a teacher or support staff member, I would learn so much about their motivations, passions, and purpose. In addition to discussing the performance standards, I started the habit of crafting five reflective questions to guide the conversation during these evaluation conferences. As I gave this more thought, I decided to replicate this process by conducting individual conversations with all staff members serving at our school. There are roughly fifty staff members on our team and I initially set out to do this monthly. After one month of doing this, I realized an individual monthly conversation with each member of our team was far too aggressive, so I adjusted this to a quarterly individual conversation. These were fifteen to thirty-minute talks centered around several questions, such as:

- Tell me about a "win" or something that has gone really well in the past few weeks.
- What do you love about your job at our school?
- If you could change one thing about our school, what would it be?
- What is your "unfair advantage" (or definite strength) that allows you to succeed on a daily basis?
- Who is someone that has been especially helpful to you that you would like to recognize?

While this is a sampling of actual questions we used, please know that these questions changed each quarter. These conversations allowed me to get to know our staff members on a deeper level while listening to their motivations, values, stories, and concerns. Purpose was established and clarified, while staff members were given a voice and felt valued. We did not solve every issue for every staff member, but time and space were created to listen and validate, which increased levels of commitment and engagement. Additionally, there were strong patterns and themes that rose to the surface. I was able to discern a sound feel for the pulse of the building, while identifying areas that needed attention.

More than likely, there are secondary administrators reading this section shaking their heads and saying, "Dan, you are crazy. Do you know how many staff members are on my team? A quarterly conversation with more than 100 people? You're nuts." I get it. Individual conversations might seem to be much more feasible at an elementary school level with fewer staff members, but we do not have to completely throw in the towel at our secondary schools. What if assistant principals shared the work to help facilitate these conversations? A quarterly conversation might be an unrealistic expectation for a secondary administrator. If that is the case, start with one per semester or even one per year. If you were able to conduct an individual conversation with each staff member on your team, there is no doubt in my mind that the level of trust in your building would be greatly enhanced. Is this challenging? Of course. Does it require a high degree of organization and discipline? Absolutely. Would it be worth it? Without question. When I think about the strategies I have employed to promote engagement in my school and district, the quarterly individual conversations have resulted in the highest impact of any by far. If you have reflective questions that you like to ask during such conversations or questions that you have been asked, please share them on your various social media outlets using the #permission2BGreat hashtag.

Push and Pull

When we think about establishing community by developing and enhancing relationships, please know it is not always about sunshine, rainbows, unicorns, and seeing the bright side of all situations. Working with and leading people is challenging work.

Burnout Behavior: Isolating when times are tough. When times get tough and challenges persist, it is somewhat natural to hunker down and keep to ourselves. Educators may isolate while keeping their nose to the grindstone when overwhelming demands continue. A large body of research has shown that other people such as colleagues, friends, and family are the greatest predictor of both performance and well-being (Achor, 2010; Lyubomirsky, 2008; Seligman, 2011). The most successful instructors invest in their friends, team members, peers, and family to drive themselves forward especially during difficult times.

Although I am a strong proponent of positive psychology, optimism, and focusing on strengths, I believe we are doing a disservice to people and being disingenuous if we do not acknowledge a certain amount of push and pull needed when leading people.

Several years ago, my oldest son was finishing up his first cycle of summer swimming lessons. All went very well for Mason until it was time for the final lesson of the year. Anyone who has taken their child to swim lessons in my community knows of the infamous *"diving board lesson."* Small children are expected to climb to the edge of the diving board, look directly in the face of their fear, and jump into the deep end of the pool. There are four-year-olds who enthusiastically run up to the board and immediately spring into the water like an exuberant dog. There are others who cry, flee, or grasp the side rails of the diving board with despair painted all over their faces. Many times, these kids must be nudged, pushed, pulled, and dragged by the instructors to complete the task. Mason Butler resembled the latter description. After a reluctant climb up the ladder and even slower drift across the board, while gripping the railing with white knuckles, I am happy to report that he did go off the diving board with just a *bit* of assistance.

As I was writing this chapter, I could not help but reflect on this situation with Mason, the diving board, and how it not only relates to the change process, but also correlates to relationship building. There is one constant in the field of education, and that constant is change. Our profession is constantly evolving with the application of new research, technology, and pedagogical practices to better serve students. The change process is often accompanied by many emotions: excitement, fear, anger, hope, and shock are just a few of the feelings educators experience as new initiatives, programs, and activities are implemented. It is often uncertain what the future will hold, causing feelings similar to what Mason experienced on the diving board.

Change is inevitable and I am certain we do not want to prevent it if we aim to achieve our personal best. In all improvement efforts, we are going to experience fear of the unknown, just like my son did on the diving board. As you continue to move forward in your improvement journey, I challenge you to embrace the fear when you find yourself on the "diving board." In the context of relationship building, understand there will be people on your team similar to the lifeguards who were in the pool supporting Mason. They will be there in the metaphorical deep end to provide safety, embrace the fall, and guide you with where you need to go. Also keep in mind, for relationships to thrive, we need "lifeguards" to provide the necessary nudge, push, or aggressive shove when times get tough. Embrace the people on your team who are there to help you become the best version of you. How many times have you avoided an awkward conversation, ignored a challenging situation, or pretended not to know something because you were uncertain or afraid of the outcome? I suspect that, like me, this has happened more than you would like to admit. Fear is wired into our brains and impossible to avoid; we must learn to dance with it and rationalize its origin. If we are experiencing fear, odds are very good we are going after something important. Dance with this fear, embrace vulnerability, establish trust, and enhance connections to best serve others.

Difficult Conversations

There are conversations that fill many leaders with fear and anxiety: the ones in which we have to deliver challenging news, talk about a sensitive topic, discuss an underperformance issue—or, simply stated, when we tell someone what they *need* to hear, as opposed to what they *want* to hear. While positive communication is of the utmost importance, effective leaders cannot shy away from conducting challenging conversations with members of their team. Here are six of my favorite tips for navigating these difficult interactions:

1. **Be Precise with Your Objectives:** Define what you want to achieve by having the conversation. Consider these questions from the research of Stone, et al. (2010): What do I hope to accomplish in this conversation? What do I need to learn? What do I need to share? Design the conversation to meet your objectives.

2. **Do Not Beat Around the Bush:** I do not believe in "sandwich feedback" when engaging in challenging conversations. When you have bad news to deliver, get to the point in a clear, concise, and kind manner. Conversations can get knocked off the rails when leaders start dancing around the issue. Get to the point with clarity and always leave your conversation partner with their dignity intact.

3. **Avoid Blame:** I recommend not engaging in the "blame game" in general, and I believe this is even more crucial to avoid during difficult conversations. The goal is not to establish who is right or who is wrong. Rather, the focus is getting to the root of the issue, while producing better outcomes in the future. Blaming will undoubtedly get in the way of making this happen. Share the issues from your point of view and listen to the concerns from their point of view as well.

4. **Summarize and Paraphrase:** As your conversation partner is talking, it is a good idea to paraphrase what they are saying every so often. This signals that you are genuinely listening while creating clarity for both parties. Two of my favorite paraphrasing statements are: "This is what I'm hearing you say…" and: "Let me summarize what I heard you say…" Taking the time to summarize and paraphrase will allow you to be in a much better position in terms of understanding your partner's perspective.

5. **Be Prepared for Negative Emotions:** Odds are good that your conversation partner will react negatively when given tough news or feedback. If you conduct enough difficult conversations, this is inevitable. While you cannot control the behavior of others, you can control your response. Stay objective and calm and make sure that you are going into the conversation in the right frame of mind. When calm, you will be much more focused and effective. If you are angry or agitated, your success rate will plummet in a hurry. In preparation, anticipate when the negative reaction may occur and be ready to respond appropriately in the moment. If you want a better outcome, you must train yourself to provide a better response.

6. **Get Curious:** There will be all kinds of thoughts going through your head during these conversations; your inner voice will be firing on all cylinders. A natural instinct is to start making assumptions, which is a conversation killer. Instead, stay curious, asking questions to gain further understanding.

1. **Asking for help** - As mentioned earlier in this chapter, educators may feel guilty asking for help for a host of reasons. I admit, oftentimes I feel like I have to take everything on myself and neglect to use the human resources around me. This, of course, is not healthy behavior and a recipe for burnout. When you have reached the point where assistance with a particular task, project, or assignment is needed, consider the following steps that will make asking for help a little easier:

   Get your mind right and swallow your pride. Everyone needs help and there are so many members of your team who are willing and able to provide you with the assistance you need. Get in the proper headspace and know that you are not alone.

   Consider the strengths of others who can best meet your needs. Think about the skills and experiences of your team members and reach out to someone who has specific skills in your area of struggle. There is always someone who can provide expertise.

   When you reach out to someone for their assistance, provide context about why you are speaking to them and how they can help you. When you provide a reason for the request, people will be even more inclined to offer their support.

2. **Learning to forgive** - As we experience challenging events and disappointment, we must learn to forgive if we are going to experience a high level of engagement. Holding onto resentment only breeds anger, frustration, and negativity. Forgiveness has been shown to decrease depression, anxiety, unhealthy anger, and the symptoms of PTSD. When we practice forgiveness we

can move forward and let the past be what it is. Here are a few tips that will help with this process:

Learning to forgive and practicing forgiveness does not mean that you are excusing the other person's behavior.

When you forgive, it doesn't mean that the emotions associated with the challenging event go away.

When you forgive, you are accepting the reality that the situation happened and you are willing to move forward.

Forgiveness is not about the other person; it is something you do for *you*. It is necessary to forgive yourself as well when you fall short of your own expectations

3. **Deliberate acts of compassion** - Research has found that committing intentional deeds of humanity decreases stress and contributes to enhanced mental health (Otake et al., 2006). By doing a kind act we become happier. The happier we feel, the more kind acts we do, and then we become even happier (Layous et al., 2012). It is a continuous cycle of positive emotion. A bonus is that we increase our social connections in this way, and other people are more inclined to be generous to us in return. The scientific research of this social investment strategy has shown that committing deliberate acts of compassion is not only good for the receiver, but also the giver (Lyubomirsky, 2008). As you consider deliberate acts of compassion, think about things that you like to do that can also help others. Maybe that involves paying for a stranger's coffee at Starbucks, helping a struggling colleague at school, or serving your community in some way. Performing a kind act will not only boost your mood but will lift the spirits of those around you.

4. **Purposeful Collaborative Meetings** - These gatherings might be called team discussions, Professional Learning Communities, or simply collaborative gatherings; what we call them is not nearly as important as what we *do* during these professional

meetings. In our school, these meetings are designed to accomplish a variety of tasks in a team setting. Within our current structure, we have dedicated time to make these grade level meetings happen once per week, complete with a theme to direct our focus. The four themes include teacher improvement plans, assessment wall check-ins, social and emotional learning discussions, and teacher choice. I encourage you to read about our structure and then develop your own ideas to infuse your meetings with purpose.

As part of the professional learning and continual growth approach in the state of Iowa, every teacher is required to complete and monitor an individual improvement plan each year. If not given the appropriate amount of focus and attention, these professional learning plans can easily become compliance assignments with limited meaning. To infuse these plans with additional life while making them more than a compliance check, we dedicate time and space each month to discuss essential individual goals, check in on progress, and monitor the specific action steps that have been put into place.

The assessment wall serves as a building-wide progress monitoring tool. All student assessment results are collected on individual cards to provide a method of displaying student progress and an efficient visual to plan future interventions. The assessment wall drives various improvement efforts and investing in the conversation around student academic needs each month has proven to be beneficial.

In addition to devoting time to discussing student academic needs through the assessment wall process, we also create opportunities to examine students' social and emotional needs each month. Our grade-level teachers participate in these conversations (led by our school counselor) which examine a variety of student needs. These needs may include support related to work completion, self-regulation, cooperation with peers, or any other need not directly related to academics. To keep the communication lines open with all supports, we include our school social worker in these meetings.

The final theme allows teachers to choose their topic of conversation. Topics can focus on anything that teachers may need at that moment in time. It is our hope that the content provided in these collaborative meetings solidifies communication and allows teachers the necessary time to fulfill vital responsibilities.

CARING for YOU

1. **"Date" nights** - Human connection matters. Educators live extremely busy lives, attempting to find a balance between school, hobbies, family responsibilities, self-care, and more. When we get overwhelmed with work demands, often our social connections fall by the wayside, but connecting with others is more important than you might think. Social connection can lower anxiety and depression, help us regulate our emotions, lead to higher self-esteem and empathy, and actually improve our immune systems (Buettner, 2017). By neglecting our need to connect, we put our health at risk. Scheduling intentional time with significant others, family, or friends is absolutely necessary. Whether it is going to dinner, taking in a movie, going bowling, taking a walk, playing a board game, or imbibing in some spirits after work, these "date night" opportunities are a great investment for increasing happiness. Organizing activities or events outside the workday to bring family, friends, and loved ones together provides the social connectedness we need to rest, recharge, and thrive. I recommend regularly scheduled

"date night" activities and staying committed to them, as the busyness of the year unfolds.

2. **Volunteer** - With active lives, it can be challenging for educators to make the time to volunteer; however, the benefits can be enormous. Not only does volunteering offer meaningful assistance to people in need and the greater community, but the right activities can also provide a host of benefits to you. Dedicating your time as a volunteer to the right-fit activity helps you make new friends, expand your network, boost your social skills and even protect your mental and physical health. The more you volunteer, the more benefits you'll experience, but volunteering need not involve a long-term commitment or consume a large amount of your day. Giving in even simple ways can help those in need and improve your health and happiness. I recommend finding an organization or an activity that fits your skills and interests to experience the full range of benefits. I love to serve as a volunteer coach for our local high school football team. I volunteer my time on Friday nights sitting in the booth, talking with our defensive coaches about game plans, strategy, and ways to win the game. On the one hand, this is a significant time commitment on my part, but is also vital to my overall self-care plan since it is something I enjoy.

Volunteering keeps you in regular contact with others and helps you develop a solid support system. Human beings are hard-wired to give to others; the more we give, the happier we feel.

CHAPTER 5

Focusing on Values
and Fairness

"Clarity is the antidote to anxiety, and therefore clarity is the preoccupation of the effective leader. If you do nothing else as a leader, be clear."
Marcus Buckingham

It was a frigid December during one of Addison's years serving as principal at two separate elementary schools. In the midst of the craziness that comes with leading two buildings simultaneously, the management aspects of the job consumed her: leaky roofs, scheduling dilemmas, student discipline concerns, supply shortages, and more. The critical instructional leadership component of the position often got buried when she was doing all the other things.

In this particular year, it seemed like the allegorical bullets really started flying in both buildings with numerous students struggling academically, behaviorally, socially, and emotionally. Addison was brought into the fold of several conversations with school counselors, instructional coaches, special education teachers, and general education teachers about the progress, or lack thereof, of these children. Carley, a fifth-grader, was overwhelmed with school expectations, work completion, self-regulation, physical aggression, and everything in between. Because of trauma she had experienced in the past, she was now experiencing social and emotional issues. Carley demonstrated consistent disrespectful behavior toward her teacher and various support staff members, struggled to regulate her emotions consistently, and negatively impacted the learning of her peers. Each day was a battle that progressively got worse, despite several interventions. It was just before the holiday season and something needed to be done or Carley, her teacher, and the entire class were not going to make it through the year.

Meanwhile, in another school on the other side of the district, Benjamin, also a fifth-grader, was struggling significantly with grade-level academic content. Benjamin was already identified for special education support; however, the subject matter and instruction delivered to him was inadequate. During previous years, the special education team increased his time to receive both core and specially-designed instruction, instituted learning accommodations and modifications, and extended paraprofessional support throughout independent and guided practice time in the classroom. Despite these efforts, his progress was minimal. The team was running out of ideas to best meet the academic needs of this student.

While Carley and Benjamin were from different schools and demonstrated completely different needs, they shared a common thread: many conversations about each were being held with a variety of staff members focused on midyear school changes to best meet the challenges they faced. Unfortunately, at the time of this story, Carley and Benjamin's school district did not have programs or specialized staff to meet the exceptional needs of all kids within each school. Instead, specific programs and expert staff were split among several buildings

across the district. While efficient, this model certainly presents challenges when kids require service outside their neighborhood school,
particularly if such a move must occur in the middle of the school
year. At the time of these events, the schools Addison was leading did
not have a behavioral resource program, nor did they have a special
education program designed to meet the needs of students requiring
more intensive levels of specially-designed instruction. Something had
to change with Carley and Benjamin. After exhausting what Addison
believed to be every option at her disposal, she had two incredibly difficult decisions to make.

No one ever wants to transition a student out of their home school
and very few parents prefer moving their child to a new learning environment, especially in the middle of the year. Routines are established,
friend groups have been developed, relationships with teachers and
staff have been formed, and families understand how the school oper-
ates. Realizing all this made Addison's decision in both schools quite
difficult. With Carley, who was demonstrating extremely disrespectful
behaviors, daily emotional and physical outbursts, and active disengagement, could the team continue to limp through the school year?
Was there anything more that the school teams could do to help turn
the corner for Carley? Would they be giving up on her? Benjamin, the
student with substantial academic concerns at the other school, was
incessantly on Addison's mind as well. She continued to wonder if
there were alternatives to meet his needs or if there was anything else
that the team could do. If a move was made, would his situation be
improved? How would Benjamin's family respond to this move? Addison was struggling to decide how best the teams could serve these two
students.

After much deliberation, Carley was moved to a new school
equipped with a behavioral resource program to better meet her various needs. While this decision pushed the team past the edge of their

comfort zones and was extremely difficult for Carley's family to accept at the time, it was the right call. She made a very smooth transition to a new school in the district and finished the year with higher levels of success and confidence than she would have experienced had Addison not made this difficult decision. Benjamin remained in his home school. The special education team worked closely with the school psychologists, and social workers to completely redesign their instructional practices. This allowed Benjamin's needs to be met for the remainder of the year before a transition to middle school occurred. The outcomes of the decisions were different (one student made a school change and the other did not); however, both choices tied back to a core value of Addison: integrity. I define integrity as doing the right thing even when it is difficult to do so. These situations pushed Addison and both teams, but knowing integrity matters deeply to them, the process was made easier. In fact, if they were faced with the same scenario many years later, they would act in an identical manner. When we gain clarity about the attributes that define us, difficult judgment calls become less difficult.

The Mismatch

School leaders everywhere are faced with decisions like Addison and her team experienced every day of their working lives. Making difficult determinations about programming, scheduling, personnel, employee discipline, parental concerns, community support, public relations, and funding are part of the job and one of the reasons leaders get paid to make them. Without a filter through which to make decisions—a North Star, or guiding light—this work can become emotionally exhausting, unnerving, and, ultimately, burn leaders out before they even get started.

Burnout Behavior: Rumination. Rumination is overthinking. With so many demands and decisions to make on any given day, it is easy to get caught in a pattern of overthinking. Rumination can result from a past experience or an upcoming event. Whether it was a parent who inappropriately yelled at you on the phone after a conflict on the bus, an upcoming presentation to the school board, or addressing a colleague about negative behavior, there are all kinds of negative consequences that arise from rumination. Overthinking can lead to sadness, foster negatively biased thinking, limit your problem solving capabilities, and impair motivation (Lyubomirsky, 2008).

However, this type of decision making is not exclusive to school leaders. Teachers, coaches, and educators alike are faced with overwhelming determinations each day as well. Should the teacher contact the parent of a fifth-grade student who continues to disclose inappropriate comments to girls in his class? Especially when the parent happens to be a district employee and has been less than enthused with previous communications of the same sort? What about the athletic coach who knows the school board member's son cannot remain in the starting lineup if her team is going to have the greatest opportunity for success? Will the coach choose honest bravery or compromise her values? Should these educators choose the popular decision to keep the peace or venture into the uncertain when the betterment of a child is on the line? What is the lens through which you look to make such important decisions? In other words, what are your personal core values? The ideals you hold close, the principles on which you rely when making critical decisions, a filter through which you experience the world? Establishing and acting on individual and organizational core values is central to creating a successful school culture that thrives in today's environment.

According to Brown (2018), "A value is a way of being or believing that we feel most important" (p. 186). Similarly, Cavanaugh (2016) claims, "Values are the things that drive you. They're what's important to you, what you stand for, what you hold dear" (p. 94). As Brown (2018) and Cavanaugh (2016) have declared, values are the fundamental beliefs and actions of a person or an organization and, thus, the motivating connection between a worker and the workplace. The stronger the "values fit" between the individual and the organization, the higher the levels of engagement. Conversely, the greater the mismatch of individual and organizational values, the greater the risk of experienced burnout.

Personal Values

What do you stand for? What do you believe in? What hill will you die on? Your responses to these questions relate to your personal values: the beliefs you hold dear, the standards that drive your decisions and behaviors, and the attitudes that define how you work and live each day. Are you aware of your personal values? To live a happy, healthy, and fulfilled life, knowing and living within your personal core values is essential. When identifying our core values, we establish a personal moral compass for making decisions with clear direction, passion, and purpose. Without narrowing this list of values, we can get lost in the noise; since everything becomes a priority, nothing is truly important. Moreover, when thinking more about these attributes to describe us, it is necessary to consider an essential question: Do we have a set of work values and home values? Brown (2018) suggests:

"We have only one set of values. We do not shift our values based on context. We are called to live in a way that is aligned with what we hold most important regardless of the setting or situation" (p. 187).

We cannot be two people. It is impossible for me to claim that I truly value integrity when in the workplace I follow all expectations and demonstrate high levels of trust but fail to honor my commitments or follow through with responsibilities at home.

Burnout Behavior: Lying to Ourselves. Throughout this chapter, I make the argument that the stronger the fit between personal and organizational values, the greater the engagement in the workplace. When engaging in this work, it is critical that we are honest with ourselves and outline the true values we stand for, we believe in, and that we hold dear. Conflict can arise when we are dishonest with ourselves and pick the wrong set of values. For example, let's suppose that I really want to be courageous as a leader and conduct difficult conversations to push our team forward, while engaging in the brave leadership that is necessary for success. I list this as a personal core value; however, when faced with the opportunities to engage in courageous conversations, I abdicate all responsibility. As much as I want to be courageous, this is not a core value at this time and I am not being truthful with myself. Behaving in this manner consistently over time will contribute to burnout.

A simple Google search for "values" yields assorted lists of personal attributes and simple activities guiding you through a process to narrow down to a critical few. Such lists can range anywhere from fifty to over two hundred characteristics and can provide a great starting point for determining what you stand for and in what you believe. I will share a list below of 148 values developed and adapted from the works of various researchers and practitioners as well as a four-step route for bringing these values to life. As you work to determine your personal core values, consider this list of characteristics developed and adapted from the works of Brown (2018), Dudley (2018), and Clear (2018):

Accomplishment	Dignity	Honesty	Love
Accountability	Discipline	Honor	Loyalty
Achievement	Diversity	Hope	Making a differ-
Adaptability	Drive	Humility	ence
Adventure	Efficiency	Humor	Mastery
Affection	Empathy	Ideals	Merit
Altruism	Empowerment	Impact	Nature
Ambition	Enthusiasm	Ingenuity	Nourishment
Authenticity	Environment	Initiative	Patriotism
Autonomy	Equality	Innovation	Peace
Balance	Ethics	Insight	Perseverance
Beauty	Excellence	Integrity	Positivity
Belonging	ExpJustintion	Intellect	Power
Career	Fairness	Intuition	Pride
Caring	Faith	Job security	Rationality
Challenge	Family	Joy	Relationships
Class	Fidelity	Justice	Resilience
Collaboration	Financial stability	Kindness	Resourcefulness
Commitment	Fitness	Knowledge	Respect
Communication	Focus	Leadership	Restraint
Community	Forgiveness	Learning	Satisfaction
Compassion	Freedom	Legacy	Security
Competence	Friendship	Leisure	Self-actualization
Competition	Fun	Love	Self-awareness
Confidence	Generosity	Loyalty	Selflessness
Connection	Goals	Mastery	Self-respect
Consciousness	Grace	Merit	Serenity
Contentment	Gratitude	Mindfulness	Service
Contribution	Grit	Money	Simplicity
Cooperation	Growth	Nature	Spontaneity
Courage	Happiness	Openness	Stability
Creativity	Hard work	Opportunity	Strength
Curiosity	Harmony	Optimism	Trust
Decisiveness	Health	Order	Truth
Dependability	Helping others	Parenting	Understanding
Determination	Inclusion	Passion	Uniqueness
Enjoyment	Independence	Patience	Vitality
			Vulnerability

Additional Values Words of Your Own Choosing:

This list of values is not intended to be comprehensive; rather, it serves as an opportunity to get started with identifying what is most important to you. As mentioned, this process will be structured into four distinct steps:

Step 1: Select All Values That Speak to You

As you look at this list of 148 values, highlight, circle, or make note of all the qualities that resonate deeply with you. You may feel inclined to highlight more than twenty values, that is completely fine. Do not scale back and feel free to add an additional descriptive trait that might not be listed.

Step 2: Reduce to Eight

At this point in the process, you will need to get more focused on the values that matter most to you. Remember, if everything is important, then nothing truly is. To help with this step, group words together and see if there is a single word that captures all the attributes of the others. For example, you may have highlighted connection, relationships, and friendship and decided that "connection" captures the essence of them all. Also, consider the following questions to help you narrow your focus:

+ What brings you joy? What do you do that leads to these positive emotions?
+ What is something that drives you crazy?
+ Think about times when you have felt accomplished and assured. What were you doing?
+ How do you spend your discretionary money?
+ Where and how do you spend your flexible time?
+ Talk to a loved one, a friend, or a trusted colleague. What would they say about the values you have selected? Would they agree?

Step 3: Final Four

After combining different values together and working through the questions to narrow your list to eight, your next step is to condense your list even further, to the four most critical values that represent you as your best self. This is difficult and to help distinguish what matters most, you will put your words up against each other in a forced decision matrix. For example, suppose two of my eight values are "accomplishment" and "connection." Place these values next to each other knowing that you can only pick one from this pair; force yourself to decide. While "accomplishment" is very important to me, "connection" wins between these two, so I will circle this on my matrix. Follow this step in the process for the remaining attributes to eventually land on four personal core values. You can see how this works by following the example below:

Your Personal Core Values
Forced Decision Matrix

Consider your eight values and why you have selected these as most important to you. Your goal within this part of the process is to condense your list from eight to four values using a forced decision matrix.

Here are your eight values:

1.	Accomplishment	4.	Empathy	7.	Self-actualization
2.	Connection	5.	Integrity	8.	Vulnerability
3.	Courage	6.	Learning		

Circle the number in each pair representing your recommended value. Total the number of times each values is circled and indicate it below.

1	2								
1	3	2	3						
1	4	2	4	3	4				
1	5	2	5	3	5	4	5		
1	6	2	6	3	6	4	6	4	7
1	7	2	7	3	7	4	7	5	7
1	8	2	8	3	8	4	8	5	8

The value with the most circles will be your top value, followed by three more to round out your top four.

1.

2.

3.

4.

How many times was each value circled as the preferred choice in each pair?

1.   2.   3.   4.   5.   6.   7.   8.

The value with the most circles will be your top value, followed by the next three to round out your top four values. Please list your top four values below (or on a separate document you are using):

Step 4: Rank Your Final Four

Now that you have determined your four personal core values, list them in order of importance to you, as indicated by the number of circles on your forced decision matrix. This order will come into play, as we work to bring these values to life in the next section. See the example of the completed forced decision matrix example. Take note that "learning" and "courage" had three votes apiece on this forced decision matrix. In the head-to-head matchup on the matrix, "learning" was more important between the two. Therefore, "learning" is #3 and "courage" is #4. I encourage you to follow the same procedure if you encounter ties in this process.

Your Personal Core Values
Forced Decision Matrix

Consider your eight values and why you have selected these as most important to you. Your goal within this part of the process is to condense your list from eight to four values using a forced decision matrix.

Here are your eight values:

1. Accomplishment
2. Connection
3. Courage
4. Empathy
5. Integrity
6. Learning
7. Self-actualization
8. Vulnerability

Circle the number in each pair representing your recommended value. Total the number of times each values is circled and indicate it below.

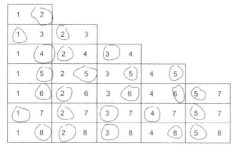

The value with the most circles will be your top value, followed by three more to round out your top four.

1. Integrity
2. Connection
3. Learning
4. Courage

How many times was each value circled as the preferred choice in each pair?

1. 2   2. 6   3. 3   4. 2   5. 7   6. 3   7. 0   8. 2

Bringing Values to Life

You have gone further than most leaders and identified your personal core values that pinpoint who you are and what is most important to you, while creating a guiding compass to direct you in challenging times. This is great news, but we are not finished. Unfortunately, many people identify their values, publish them on an attractive card or poster, place them on the wall in a prominent location, and never refer to them again. This is not only a mistake, but also a missed opportunity to live our best life. In the next portion of this chapter, in addition to listing the top four values, we will produce unique definitions for them, create and answer daily questions to hold ourselves accountable, and develop personal strategies to bring the values to life.

Define Your Values

Now that you have identified your four personal core values, it is important to create your own definitions. What do these values mean to you? Creating clarity with your own definition of these values increases the likelihood of staying true to them. In the example below, I define "connection" as a commitment to investing in people, while giving of myself to them. Dudley (2018) recommends beginning your definition with "A commitment to" followed by a clearly defined action. You will notice that I have followed this advice in the examples. Keep in mind, by creating personal definitions of our values, we are striving for clarity, not literary genius. In other words, do not overthink it.

After you have established a definition of your values, you will then craft a daily question to ask yourself at the beginning or end of each day. This practice is also inspired from Dudley's work (2018). He recommends three key characteristics of action-driving questions:

1. It cannot be answered yes or no; it must demand that you identify what you did and how you did it.
2. It should not include the actual value in the question.
3. It must provide flexibility in how it can be answered. (p. 211).

A daily question related to connection might be: "What did I do today to make someone's day just a little bit better?" As you can see, this question cannot be answered with a simple yes or no. The question does not include the word "connection" and can be answered in many ways. Daily questions are designed to hold ourselves accountable to living out our personal core values.

Now that you have identified your top four core values, produced your own definition, and crafted a question to hold yourself responsible for living out these values, it is imperative to list individual tactics, strategies, or activities to truly bring these values to life. In the example below, you will notice three actions designed to help in living out the "connection" value: spending intentional time with loved ones, writing notes of appreciation, and giving time to others for the purpose of service. Following this process as shown in the example will allow you to stay true to who you are as your best self. Personal core values provide the guiding light to take your leadership to a higher level. It may appear overwhelming when thinking about monitoring all four of your personal core values daily. As you engage in this work, I encourage you to direct your focus to just one value at first. This will set you up for success, while not making the process quite as intense. Once you have your feet under you, monitor more values using this process. The goal is not to make this laborious; rather, to direct your focus to becoming the best version of yourself.

Personal Core Values

(1) Clearly define each of your values. Start each definition with "A commitment to" which will almost always be followed with a verb.

(2) Operationalize each value by turning it into an action-oriented question you can answer daily.

(3) The *Personal Tactics* column is intended to bring the value to life by listing everyday actions you can accomplish that help you live in alignment with your value.

VALUE	DEFINITION	DAILY QUESTION	PERSONAL TACTICS
Integrity	*Integrity* is a commitment to doing the right thing even when doing so is difficult.	What did I do today that was difficult, but the right thing to do?	• Make daily decisions consistent with my values. • Do what I say I will do; honor all commitments. • Always tell the truth.
Connection	Connection is a commitment to investing in people, while giving of myself to them.	What did I do to make someone's day just a little bit better?	• Spend intentional time with loved ones. • Write notes of appreciation. • Give my time to others for the purpose of service.
Learning	Learning is a commitment to growth, exploring topics out of my comfort zone, and seeking feedback.	What did I learn today?	• Read every day for at least fifteen minutes. • Listen to podcasts. • Seek feedback from trusted colleagues and loved ones.

VALUE	DEFINITION	DAILY QUESTION	PERSONAL TACTICS
Courage	Courage is a commitment to action even when I am unsure of the outcome.	What did I do today that posed a risk or made me vulnerable, yet I tried it anyway?	+ Conduct difficult conversations when needed. + Discuss necessary issues with family members. + Challenge colleagues to grow.

Organizational Values

If schools and districts aim to perform at their highest levels, it is critical to establish a comparable level of values clarity beyond the individual level. As a school or district, what do we stand for? What drives our daily decisions? What do we feel deep within our core? In essence, what is the culture we are looking to establish within our organization? Culture is a term thrown around loosely in the educational context to the point of becoming a mere buzzword. Establishing a positive culture is vital and impacts every component of the school environment; however, what exactly does it mean?

Culture

When you walk into a school you can sense the culture. Whether it is the initial interaction with a school secretary when walking through the office doors, observing décor on the walls, listening to conversations in the hallways among staff members, observing the principal leading professional learning with teachers, or seeing faculty engage with students, all these experiences elicit emotions and provide strong indicators of the school culture. But what exactly is school culture? Common phrases include:

+ The way things are done around here.
+ The underlying norms that direct plans and decisions.
+ The written and unwritten rules.

While I like pieces of these familiar descriptions, I favor the clarity Tim Kight provides regarding culture. The founder and CEO of *Focus 3* describes culture as three things:

1. What a group of people believe,
2. How they behave, and
3. The experience they deliver to others and receive in return (Kight, 2020).

Belief, behavior, and experience. Now I will describe a process to define the culture, while leaning into our collective core values.

Shared Core Values

The stronger the fit between the values of educators and the values of the school or district, the higher the levels of positive energy, involvement, and efficacy will result. Conversely, the greater the discrepancy between individual and collective core values, the greater the risk for emotional exhaustion, cynicism, and ineffectiveness. In more than a decade as a school administrator, I have held this belief close to my heart, yet struggled mightily designing a successful method of establishing meaningful core values for the organizations I have served. During my time as a principal, I have invested much time, effort, and energy with staff members brainstorming on sticky notes, arranging phrases into themes, thinking of extravagant words to describe who we are—all with limited success. The core values we established looked great on a poster but were lifeless.

Burnout Behavior: Poster-Worthy Values. As we engage in defining our individual and organizational core values, it can be easy to spend countless hours making sure core values include just the right words, while appearing visually attractive to the general public. There is nothing wrong with displaying attractive posters in prominent locations listing what the organization values. However, when more time is spent making something pretty than defining the actions associated with the values, we have a problem. You can have just the right words for your organizational values, but if the daily actions of your people don't match the poster, disengagement is certain.

We were spending time defining and publishing our core values, but it was not moving the needle to the extent we had hoped it would.

After reading *The Advantage: Why Organizational Health Trumps Everything Else in Business* by Patrick Lencioni (2012), I devised a much better process to identify the core values that truly represent our school, while producing behaviors that drive success. Lencioni poses a simple question for leaders to consider when working with their teams: What makes us unique? I posed this question to all staff members to begin the new school year. The purpose of this question is to list the traits that set our school apart from others, identifying the positive qualities of our school that could not be denied. In other words, our core values. The responses were incredibly consistent, some of which included: *"The people...staff, kids, and families...I love the people that make up our school...We have a mission to stay positive. Hard things will come our way, but we work hard and stay positive through it all...Our people—they very quickly have become family! I look forward to my future children attending here one day...The dedication every staff member has to making every student's school experience positive...Our continued growth, and fun!"*

I then sifted through all the responses and conducted follow up conversations with staff members. During this process, themes emerged and we created a statement that distinguishes our school from other schools. The statement declares who we are as a school, while clearly listing what is valued within the building:

*At Epworth Elementary, we place a **high value on people**. **Positive relationships** with students, colleagues, and families are of the utmost importance. We believe in **genuine communication**, while providing a **welcoming atmosphere** focused on teamwork, growth, and fun.*

As you read this statement, you can see the words or phrases in bold-type that represent our four core values: high value on people, positive relationships, genuine communication, and welcoming atmosphere. These core values have been in place long before I was the principal of the school and will be around for many years to come. These attributes are woven into the fabric of our school and live in the hearts and minds of people connected to our building. As you engage in this work related to organizational values, it is important to consider a variation of values.

Value Variations

True core values rarely change over time and steer every facet of the organization. Hiring decisions, employee discipline matters, incentives, communication, and all other aspects of school operations align directly to the core values in a thriving culture. As mentioned above, core values already exist in the organization; they are not something a school or district desires to be. Instead, those are what Lencioni (2012) refers to as "aspirational values." Suppose a school is interested in becoming more innovative with the use of recently secured mobile devices for their students. Prior to receiving these devices, the school employed largely traditional instructional practices. Now that they have received these devices for their students, they are interested in becoming much more innovative. Being innovative is something this school is *aiming* to be, not something they *are*. This is an important distinction when identifying core values within the organization. Furthermore, Lencioni (2012) describes two other variations that he calls "accidental" values and "permission to play" values.

Accidental values, as the term suggests, just kind of happen. For example, without consciously thinking about it, the last ten hires at a high school happened to be mothers who range in age from 27-35. It is understandable that the candidate pool may be limited and these are the best candidates for the advertised positions; however, an unintended consequence of these decisions is that the last ten teachers hired in this building are very similar to each other, at least in terms of certain demographic variables. This might not be a bad thing; in fact, it might be a very good thing. However, it is an unintended consequence, therefore becoming an "accidental value." When posting a position for a high school teacher, we are not openly searching for only mothers in a particular age range. The key take-away is we must be intentional about the decisions we make in our schools, ensuring they tie back to the core values of the building or district.

The final variation of values that Lencioni (2012) describes may be the most common: "Permission to play" values. Permission to play values are the minimum standards of behavior that often get confused with core values. I coached high school baseball for many years. When we showed up to play a double header, it was expected that we would have helmets, bats, gloves, catcher's equipment, and baseballs to play the game. Without these basic necessities, we would be unable to take the field. It works the same way in organizational culture. You will find words like "respect" and "honesty" as part of many values statements and strategic plans, when visiting all kinds of organizations. These values are the equivalent of the baseball equipment described above and fall into the "permission to play" category. While necessary in any successful organization, it goes without saying (one hopes) that respect and honesty are highly valued. It is assumed that anyone joining the team will be respectful and truthful; such fundamental characteristics are a necessary ticket in the door.

The Rallying Cry

After clearly articulating core values, we must then create goals to determine the most important priority right now. The "rallying cry" is a statement that determines what will direct the team's focus for the next three-to-twelve months. Once again, this process and the associated terminology comes from the work of Lencioni (2012). While establishing a rallying cry, or thematic goal, consider the following critical question: If we accomplish one thing in the next three to twelve months, what will it be? Most schools establish several strategic goals over the years. Some of these goals are achieved and others are not. The difference can often be attributed to lack of clarity or focus.

To promote a clarity of focus as we began a new school year, I asked our staff members the following question: "As you think about the approaching school year, what do you feel is our top priority as a building? Without a top priority, everything becomes important and we end up reacting to whatever issues seem urgent at the time." The responses I received were incredibly consistent and you will find two examples here:

- *"I think priority number one is helping our students to feel safe this year. Academic success is important, but their emotional well-being during this time is something that will affect them for years to come,"*
- *"Providing a safe and loving environment where we can meet both the emotional and educational needs of our students (both virtual and in person)."*

It should be noted that this question was posed to our staff members days before returning to school amid the COVID-19 Pandemic. Like most schools across the United States, our school was closed from March 16, 2020 through the beginning of June with no school in the summer months as well. When students began the new school year, they had been away from us for five and a half months. It was not a surprise to see so many responses related to the social and emotional well-being of our kids. I examined the responses and conducted follow up conversations with staff members to compose the following "rallying cry" to guide us moving forward in the upcoming school year: *"During the 2020-2021 school year, we will provide a healthy, safe, and loving environment where the social, emotional, and educational needs of all students and staff can be met."*

Returning to school in a face-to-face format in the middle of a global pandemic was sure to test us and it most certainly did. This rallying cry was critical to keeping the entire staff focused on what mattered most.

Blank Individual Example

WHO ARE WE?

At Epworth Elementary, we place a high value on people. Positive relationships with students, colleagues, and families are of the utmost importance. We believe in genuine communication, while providing a welcoming atmosphere focused on teamwork, growth, and fun.

OUR RALLYING CRY

During the 2020–2021 school year, we will provide a healthy, safe, and loving environment where the social, emotional, and educational needs of all students and staff can be met.

DEFINING OBJECTIVES OF THE RALLYING CRY

STANDARD OBJECTIVES TO KEEP ME GOING

As you look at the blank rally cry sheet, you will notice two lines of objectives with blank boxes and circles below. The first row is filled with four boxes of defining objectives that will be filled with actionable steps that, when completed, will help the individual achieve the rallying cry. Regardless of the position in which you serve at your school, this goal-setting process works the same. The circles underneath the boxes will be filled with black, gray, or white colors. Black indicates that you are on track and doing well in meeting this action; gray means that you are making progress, but not nailing it; and white reveals that you have more work to do. Ideally, you would check in on these defining objectives weekly; however, this is a monthly task for most people serving in our school. Next, you will see an example of my individual plan complete with the action steps in the defining objectives section. You will also see my progress during this month by paying attention to the colors of the circles underneath the boxes. These four defining objectives established a level of focus that I needed to get the year started successfully, while contributing to what our building was aiming to achieve. It should be noted that the defining objectives can change. This document is intended to provide a high degree of clarity, while being flexible at the same time.

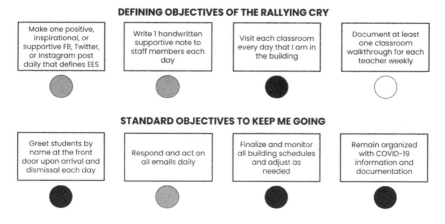

WHO ARE WE?

At Epworth Elementary, we place a high value on people. Positive relationships with students, colleagues, and families are of the utmost importance. We believe in genuine communication, while providing a welcoming atmosphere focused on teamwork, growth, and fun.

OUR RALLYING CRY

During the 2020-2021 school year, we will provide a healthy, safe, and loving environment where the social, emotional, and educational needs of all students and staff can be met.

DEFINING OBJECTIVES OF THE RALLYING CRY

| Make one positive, inspirational, or supportive FB, Twitter, or Instagram post daily that defines EES | Write 1 handwritten supportive note to staff members each day | Visit each classroom every day that I am in the building | Document at least one classroom walkthrough for each teacher weekly |

STANDARD OBJECTIVES TO KEEP ME GOING

| Greet students by name at the front door upon arrival and dismissal each day | Respond and act on all emails daily | Finalize and monitor all building schedules and adjust as needed | Remain organized with COVID-19 information and documentation |

Next, you will see an example from one of our teachers. It is important to note that the defining objectives to meet the rallying cry are steps intended to go above and beyond what is normally done as part of your typical responsibilities.

WHO ARE WE?

At Epworth Elementary, we place a high value on people. Positive relationships with students, colleagues, and families are of the utmost importance. We believe in genuine communication, while providing a welcoming atmosphere focused on teamwork, growth, and fun.

OUR RALLYING CRY

During the 2020-2021 school year, we will provide a healthy, safe, and loving environment where the social, emotional, and educational needs of all students and staff can be met.

DEFINING OBJECTIVES OF THE RALLYING CRY

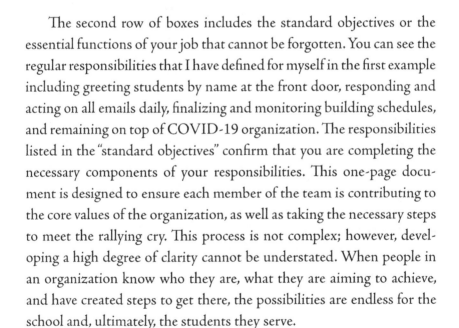

Make connection with each child every day (eye contact, use their name, positive comment)	Teach, model, and practice self-regulation skills with all groups	Run the technical side of live announcements and promote staff participation	Have frequent check-ins with colleagues about their well-being
●	●	○	◐

STANDARD OBJECTIVES TO KEEP ME GOING

Organize and plan engaging content with appropriate accommodations and differentiation	Respond and act on all emails daily	Communicate at least weekly with all families regarding good news and challenging news	Fulfill my role and responsibilities on the PBIS committee
●	●	◐	○

The second row of boxes includes the standard objectives or the essential functions of your job that cannot be forgotten. You can see the regular responsibilities that I have defined for myself in the first example including greeting students by name at the front door, responding and acting on all emails daily, finalizing and monitoring building schedules, and remaining on top of COVID-19 organization. The responsibilities listed in the "standard objectives" confirm that you are completing the necessary components of your responsibilities. This one-page document is designed to ensure each member of the team is contributing to the core values of the organization, as well as taking the necessary steps to meet the rallying cry. This process is not complex; however, developing a high degree of clarity cannot be understated. When people in an organization know who they are, what they are aiming to achieve, and have created steps to get there, the possibilities are endless for the school and, ultimately, the students they serve.

Does This Really Matter?

You may be asking yourself, "Does this really matter; is it worth all the effort?" Before you answer that question, allow me to share two stories about culture and how it can act as an invisible force to dictate behavior.

Upon graduation from college, I worked as a long-term substitute teacher in an alternative school setting for eight months. This was a stressful job working with middle and high school students who had been removed from the public-school environment for fighting, severe truancy, drug use, and/or possession of firearms at school. I was new, innocent, naïve, and focused on connecting with my students. And I set out to "fix" them. As my colleagues and I struggled through situations in which my students were verbally and physically aggressive, I quickly noticed this was going to be more challenging than I thought. I could feel the tension in the voices of fellow staff members when I engaged with them and could see the emotional exhaustion on their faces and in their body language.

A universal coping mechanism not for some, but all staff members at this school, was smoking cigarettes. During their time away from students, they would go outside to light up. As I felt the emotional toll of the job in the first month, I followed suit and started smoking. This was never something I had done in the past. In fact, I saw my mother constantly battle with nicotine addiction throughout my childhood and could not understand why people would start doing this, yet here I was, striking up like everyone else at the facility. There was an invisible force at play shaping my behavior: the culture was dictating how I should act. Let me be very clear: I am in charge of my own decisions and no one at this alternative school was outwardly pressuring me to smoke. Yet the culture of the organization was constantly signaling to me, "This is what we do to relieve stress."

School, district, and organizational culture consistently influences the behavior of individuals across the globe. Consider another story about a veteran teacher who recently made a move to a new school. In the past, this teacher and her grade-level team had a well-known reputation of openly complaining in collaborative meetings, regularly blaming parents for all student concerns, and demonstrating negative behavior at every turn. The culture of this teacher's former building not only tolerated this conduct, but inadvertently encouraged these actions.

Burnout Behavior: Avoiding Difficult Conversations. We've all been there. Perhaps a team member hasn't been holding up their end of the bargain in collaborative meetings, maybe a colleague is not meeting performance expectations, or a staff member continues to make rude comments in professional learning sessions. Whatever the situation or scenario, undoubtedly, we all have experiences where we need to talk to someone about uncomfortable topics. These conversations are often avoided in the educational context for a variety of reasons and the hope is that the issue will resolve itself. I am just as guilty as the next person regarding difficult conversations. There have been many missed opportunities in my career to address an issue directly. While we hope the conflict will get resolved on its own, this is rarely the case. When difficult conversations are avoided, this is a recipe for rumination, resentment, and ultimately, burnout.

The leaders of the school failed to address the negative behavior; rather, they gave this protesting group of teachers fewer responsibilities in hopes that their attitudes would change. Guess what? Mindsets did not change. In fact, the opposite happened, as these teachers were unwittingly being rewarded for their counterproductive actions.

In the new building, where the established core values of the school focused on relationships, collaboration, vulnerability, and teamwork, this teacher was celebrated as a colleague full of positive energy, enthusiasm, and confidence. What changed? Obviously, this teacher was placed in a different environment with a highly effective leader and a positive staff. Although these physical changes were noticeable, what mattered more was the new culture. A critical component of culture is communicating core values that will drive successful behaviors. Without engaging in this critical work, we risk operating in a default setting, which may result in an unproductive, dysfunctional, or even dangerous workplace.

As for myself, I am happy to report that I stopped smoking when I no longer worked at this alternative school facility. I am grateful for the experience, though, as it helped me become aware of the strong invisible influence of organizational culture. As we work in schools and districts, we must realize the importance of establishing a culture focused on energy, involvement, and efficacy. Creating a thriving culture begins with developing exceptional clarity around individual and organizational core values.

1. **Address Rumination** - As previously mentioned in this chapter, with so much information coming to educators at a rapid pace, rumination (overthinking) can occur rather easily. Establishing clarity around personal values can certainly help with rumination; however, here are a few more practical strategies to address it in the moment. Distract yourself from overwhelming, swirling thoughts. It is best to choose activities that you enjoy, provoke curiosity, or make you proud. Some of my favorite distractions include:

   a. Calling a loved one

   b. Cleaning my house/organizing my closet or work area

c. Listening to a podcast

d. Watching a movie

e. Reading a book

f. Taking a walk or running on the treadmill

Another important strategy is to outline a logical first step to address your problem. For example, maybe you are ruminating about a parent phone call that you took earlier in the day and can't seem to get this out of your head. What is the first logical step to address the problem? Perhaps it makes sense to write down some of the key points of the conversation that might need clarification. Or maybe it's sharing some of the information with your supervisor while seeking advice. Whatever the situation, take the first step. I like to act more and think less when wrestling with rumination.

2. **Personality Assessments** - *Strengthsfinder 2.0* is a brief, but excellent book by Tom Rath (2007) from Gallup and comes with a unique code to an online assessment to determine your top five strengths. There are 177 questions that take about forty-five minutes to complete. Each question has a time limit of twenty seconds, which forces you to answer with your initial instinct. After the assessment has been completed, a report will be provided complete with five strengths, descriptions, and action plans to develop each of these assets. This is a very useful tool, especially if you are interested in learning more about yourself and how you interact with others, while digging into your individual core values.

The *Enneagram* is an exemplary framework designed to provide insights into individuals, groups, and collectives. The *Enneagram* uncovers patterns of behavior that subconsciously drive and motivate us to act in certain ways through an online assessment. Understanding what drives us allows us to better understand ourselves and to consciously choose different behaviors than we might naturally choose. While there are similarities between *Enneagram* and *Strengthsfinder*, *Enneagram* provides additional personality data. This is another great tool for learning more about ourselves, what we value, and how we potentially relate to others in team settings. Additional information about the *Enneagram* can be found at: https://www.integrative9.com/, as well as a free online assessment at: https://www.yourenneagramcoach.com/. (You can use the QR codes below to access):

There are many other personality assessments, of course. The key is to find something that helps you to determine what matters most to you, while getting a strong sense of your core values.

3. **Best Possible Self Activity** - The best possible self-activity consists of a brief writing exercise in which you imagine your best possible self in the future when your goals have been met (King, 2001). Take a few minutes to visualize your best self in the areas of career, relationships, hobbies, and health and write a description with as much detail as you like.

To begin this exercise, find a place where you will be undisturbed for a few minutes. Select a time in the future—it could be five years from now, or three months from now. Imagine yourself in that future where things have gone right. Perhaps you are flourishing as a teacher, your family is healthy and happy, your debt has been paid off, and you are building a strong savings account. The point is to visualize your best possible future that is attainable in reality.

Now spend ten minutes writing a description of that future self with as much detail as you like. As you write, don't get hung up on spelling or grammatical errors; rather, direct your focus to writing about your future self-achieving these big goals. The exercise has been shown to clarify core values, boost people's positive emotions, happiness levels, optimism, hope, and elevate positive expectations about the future.

4. **Your One Word** - Inspired by the work of Jon Gordon, Dan Britton, and Jimmy Page (2013), this activity is designed to produce a word to define your vision and focus for the school year. This activity is like the personal values exercise that we worked through at the beginning of the chapter, with the difference being a narrowing down of your focus to a single word. It is necessary to find a word that inspires you to be better and something you can keep referring to in challenging times.

1. **Take time for yourself** - As an educator, your primary job is to serve others, which causes you to put the needs of others before your own needs quite often. If you are a parent or providing care to someone outside of your school, then these demands are

replicated when you step foot into your home. If we are going to perform at our absolute best, we need to dedicate attention to our own needs. In my experiences, educators wait far too long to make time for themselves. Quite often, they tend to wait until they are on the verge of a breakdown before realizing they need some time away from everyone else. My suggestion is to make time for yourself each day. This doesn't need to be extravagant, but it does need to be consistent. This time could be a quiet ten minutes organizing materials in your office before leaving for the day, a warm bath after the kids are in bed, fifteen minutes of solitude on your drive home, quiet reading on your front porch, or silent reflection in the morning before anyone else is up in the house. Be on the lookout for small moments in your day; there are empty spaces in almost every day that you can inhabit in solitude. Your need to replenish is as important as your need to get through your daily tasks. As you regularly engage in this practice, I am convinced you will be clearer on what matters most.

2. **Technology fasting** - Technology tools are a critical component in today's educational environment, as they allow us to work more efficiently and connect from a distance. Nonetheless, without careful attention, these tools can consume educators, allowing us to never be "away" from school. Whether we are checking emails on our phones, posting an update to a school Facebook page, or communicating via a mass text message to school families, our technology tools and applications are more accessible than ever. This is great, until it starts interfering with life responsibilities outside of school. The boundary lines between work and home have been drastically blurred due to the advancement and accessibility of technology tools. To combat this issue, I no longer have email

access on my phone, and have encouraged our teaching staff to remove it as well. This allows me to resist the urge to check email when I am away from school. As mentioned in Chapter 2, I have established a communication protocol with staff members, which helps me to be more present in the moment. Consider establishing boundaries or periodically fasting from your technology tools.

Conclusion

"If one advances confidently in the direction of his/her dreams, and endeavors to live the life which (s)he has imagined, (s)he will meet with a success unexpected in common hours."

Henry David Thoreau

It was the fall of 2002 and I was coaching freshman football at a nearby high school. Fresh out of college and student teaching at a local elementary school during the day, I thought I was a big deal for getting paid to coach football at my alma mater. I was a typical first-year coach: enthusiastic, arrogant, and ready to tell these old school Hall of Fame coaches how things should be done. There was an unforgettable boy on our team named Robbie who was small, slow, and not much of a football player. Robbie did not see the field much during his freshman year. Having all the answers at the age of twenty-two, I wrote Robbie off in my mind. I remember talking negatively about him and other players during coaches' meetings: "This kid will never be a player for us. He's slow, soft, and not someone who will contribute much to this program."

October rolled around and we finished the season with a dismal 3-6 record, thanks, at least in part, to my ineffective coaching methods. I ate a big piece of humble pie that year and realized maybe I did not know everything there was to know about defensive schemes or motivating young men. I came back the following three seasons to see

Robbie progress dramatically as he moved through the program. He grew four inches between his freshman and sophomore seasons and started seeing the field a little more, but was still not a key contributor on his team. As a junior, Robbie grew to be 6'1" and earned a starting spot on the varsity team as a wide receiver. Still, he caught only three passes the entire season. Something significant happened between Robbie's junior and senior seasons. He was now 6'3", tipped the scales at 175 pounds of solid, lean muscle, and became one of the fastest runners on the team. The kid who "would never be a player for us" was running a forty-yard dash in 4.6 seconds with a vertical jump well over twenty-five inches, and developed a fierce, competitive attitude to boot. Robbie dedicated himself to the weight room, extra repetitions in practice, and disciplined nutrition to prepare for an exceptional season.

During Robbie's senior season, he led our conference in receptions, was recognized as the Most Valuable Player on his team by his peers, earned First Team All-Conference accolades, was selected to play in the Iowa Shrine Bowl game, and earned First Team All-Area honors. Basically, if there was a post season award, Robbie earned it his senior year. Three years earlier this kid could barely run on the field without falling over his feet and had now developed into an elite athlete in the state of Iowa.

The end of Robbie's senior season slapped me directly across the face. As I attended the award ceremonies and banquets at which he was recognized for all his achievements, I realized how ridiculous I had been three years earlier. I completely wrote this kid off before he fully developed. I was judgmental, ignorant, and unfair. Robbie did not hear my comments in the coach's meetings, but he undoubtedly detected my body language when I was in his presence. At that defining moment, I decided I would never give up on a kid or an adult again. You never know when something is going to click. There are kids like Robbie sitting in our classrooms and similar situations with adults working at our schools right now. There are students who have not found their niche and educators who may have lost their way. There are other people who have not found or have forgotten what motivates them. After experiencing this situation with Robbie, I realized you never know when the switch is going to flip and we can never give up hope on a fellow human being. At this challenging time in our profession, we cannot give up on our students or colleagues. We must continue to invest in them to create systems of positive energy, involvement, and efficacy. The leadership lessons I learned from Robbie that year humbled me, but will stay with me for a lifetime.

Are You a Leader?

When you hear the term "leader", does the default setting in your mind go to the same place as mine? Many larger-than-life figures in history, such as Abraham Lincoln, Martin Luther King, Jr., Eleanor Roosevelt, or more recently, Jeff Bezos, Oprah Winfrey, and Melinda Gates, are often at the center of the conversation when considering the concept of leadership. Our society and media outlets have contributed to these patterns by showcasing leadership as this illustrious endeavor reserved for a select few. In the eyes of some, to be a leader means you must have a number of initials behind your name in an email signature, a title with "Director" or "Officer" attached to it, or situated around a large table making high-stakes decisions. While these examples certainly do describe some leaders and leadership, there is so much more in our everyday actions and interactions that make us leaders.

I define a leader as anyone who positively influences others and motivates them to be better. When working from that definition, I believe we all have the capacity to influence workload, control, and autonomy; enhance encouragement, recognition, and appreciation; build community and improve relationships; and establish a high level of clarity while living out the principles shared in this book. When the conditions are right, we all can lead the way, working intentionally to extinguish burnout, while improving engagement in our schools. Countless educators exhibit greatness countless times per day at schools and districts across the country. It is my firm belief that small, intentional acts of everyday leadership consistently committed over time can significantly improve our educational system and the opportunities we provide our students.

My fourth-grade teacher, Mrs. Lammers, saw something in me that I was unable to see in myself when she granted me permission to be great many years ago. There are kids in our classrooms and educators serving them in schools across the globe who are not yet able to comprehend their influence. It does not matter to me what role you fulfill in the educational setting. Whether you are a paraprofessional, school secretary, teacher, assistant principal, food service worker, superintendent, bus driver, principal, or custodian, you have the ability to enhance relationships with students and colleagues, improve communication with your team, establish clarity in your role, and demonstrate resilience in the face of daily challenges—all while investing in of yourself. Between these intentional acts and the practices outlined in this book, you are equipped to give others the best gift they can ever receive: *Permission to be great*. *You* are a leader, and we need *you*.

References

Achor, S. (2010). *The happiness advantage: The seven principles of positive psychology that fuel success and performance at work.* Crown Business.

Arens, A. K., & Morin, A. J. S. (2016). Relations between teachers' emotional exhaustion and students' educational outcomes. *Journal of Educational Psychology, 108*(6), 800–813. https://doi.org/10.1037/edu0000105

Bakker, A. B., & Demerouti, E. (2007). The job demands-resources model: State of the art. *Journal of Managerial Psychology, 22*(3), 309–328. https://doi.org/10.1108/02683940710733115

Barnes, G., Crowe, E., & Schaefer, B. (2007). *The cost of teacher turnover in five school districts: A pilot study.* National Commission on Teaching and America's Future.

Brown, B. (2018). *Dare to lead: Brave work. Tough conversations. Whole hearts.* Random House.

Buettner, D. (2017). *The blue zones of happiness: Lessons from the world's happiest people.* National Geographic Partners.

Cavanaugh, A. (2016). *Contagious culture: Show up, set the tone, and intentionally create an organization that thrives.* McGraw Hill Education.

Chapman, G., & White, P. (2019). *The 5 languages of appreciation in the workplace: Empowering organizations by encouraging people* (3rd ed.). Northfield Publishing.

Christakis, N., & Fowler, J. H. (2011). *Connected: The surprising power of our social networks and how they shape our lives-how your friends' friends' friends affect everything you feel, think, and do.* Little, Brown and Company.

Clear, J. (2018). *Atomic habits: An easy & proven way to build good habits & break bad ones.* Penguin.

Cockerell, L. (2015). *Time management magic: How to get more done every day and move from surviving to thriving.* Emerge.

Coyle, D. (2018). *The culture code: The secrets of highly successful groups.* Bantam.

Csikszentmihalyi, M. (1997). *Finding flow: The psychology of engagement with everyday life.* Basic Books.

Dudley, D. (2018). *This is day one: A practical guide to leadership that matters.* Hachett Books.

Fredrickson, B. (2009). *Positivity: Groundbreaking reveals how to embrace the hidden strength of positive emotions, overcome negativity, and thrive.* Crown Publishers.

Goleman, D. (2006). *Social intelligence: The new science of human relationships.* Bantam Books.

Gordon, J., Britton, D., & Page, J. (2013). *One word that will change your life.* Wiley.

Haidt, J. (2006). *The happiness hypothesis: Finding modern truth in ancient wisdom.* Basic Books.

Halbesleben, J. R. B. (2010). A meta-analysis of work engagement: Relationships with burnout, demands, resources, and consequences. In M. P. Leiter & A. B. Bakker (Eds.), *Work engagement: A handbook of essential theory and research* (pp. 102–117). Psychology Press.

Heath, C., & Heath, D. (2010). *Switch: How to change things when change is hard.* Broadway Books.

Ingersoll, R., Merrill, L., Stuckey, D., & Collins, G. (2018). Seven trends: The transformation of the teaching force (RR 2018 – 2). Consortium for

Policy Research in Education. https://repository.upenn.edu/cgi/viewcontent.cgi?article=1109&context=cpre_researchreports

Kight, T. (2020). "Culture Playbook: Energize Winning Behavior." *Focus 3,* 15 Sept. 2020, focus3.com/training/culture-playbook/.

King L. (2001). The health benefits of writing about life goals. Personality and Social Psychology Bulletin. 27(7), 798-807. https://doi.org/10.1177%2F0146167201277003

Knight, J. (2012). *High impact instruction: A framework for great teaching.* Corwin Press.

Knight, J. (2014). *Focus on teaching: Using video for high-impact instruction.* Corwin Press.

Layous, K., Nelson, S. K., Oberle, E., Schonert-Reichl, K. A., & Lyubomirsky, S. (2012). Kindness counts: Prompting prosocial behavior in preadolescents boosts peer acceptance and well-being. *PLoS ONE, 7*(12), 1–3. https://doi.org/10.1371/journal.pone.0051380

Leiter, M. P., & Maslach, C. (2005). *Banishing burnout: Six strategies for improving your relationship with work.* Jossey-Bass.

Lencioni, P. (2012). *The advantage: Why organizational health trumps everything else in business.* Jossey-Bass.

Lyubomirsky, S. (2008). *The how of happiness: A new approach to getting the life you want.* Penguin Books.

Maslach, C., & Leiter, M. P. (1997). *The truth about burnout: How organizations cause personal stress and what to do about it.* Jossey-Bass.

Maslach, C., & Leiter, M. P. (2016). Understanding the burnout experience: Recent research and its implications for psychiatry. *World Psychiatry, 15*(2), 103–111. https://doi.org/10.1002/wps.20311

Maslach, C., Schaufeli, W. B., & Leiter, M. P. (2001). Job burnout. *Annual Review of Psychology, 52*(1), 397–422. https://doi.org/10.1146/annurev.psych.52.1.397

McGregor, D. (1960). The human side of enterprise. McGraw-Hill.

Medina, J. (2014). *Brain rules: 12 principles for surviving and thriving at work, home, and school* (2nd ed.). Pear Press.

Meyer U., & Coffee, W. (2015). *Above the line: Lessons in leadership and life from a championship season.* Penguin Press.

Otake, K., Shimai, S., Tanaka-Matsumi, J., Otsui, K., & Fredrickson, B. L. (2006). Happy people become happier through kindness: A counting kindnesses intervention. *Journal of Happiness Studies, 7*(3), 361–375. https://doi.org/10.1007/s10902-005-3650-z

Pfeffer, J. (2018). *Dying for a paycheck: How modern management harms employee health and company performance-and what you can do about it.* Harper Collins

Pink, D. (2009). *Drive: The surprising truth about what motivates us.* Riverhead Books.

Ratey, J. J., & Hagerman, E. (2013). *Spark: The revolutionary new science of exercise and the brain.* Little, Brown and Company.

Rath, T. (2007). Strengthsfinder 2.0. Gallup Press.

Seligman, M. E. P. (2011). *Flourish: A visionary new understanding of happiness and well-being.* Atria.

Slatcher, R. B., & Pennebaker, J. W. (2006). How do I love thee? let me count the words: The social effects of expressive writing. *Psychological Science, 17*(8), 660–664. https://doi.org/10.1111/j.1467-9280.2006.01762.x

Steinhardt, M. A., Jaggars, S. E. S., Faulk, K. E., & Gloria, C. T. (2011). Chronic work stress and depressive symptoms: Assessing the mediating role of teacher burnout. *Stress and Health, 27*(5), 420–429. https://doi.org/10.1002/smi.1394

Stone, D., Patton, B., Heen, S. (2010). *Difficult conversations: How to discuss what matters most.* Penguin Books.

Stickgold, R., Malia, A., Maguire, D., Roddenberry, D., & O'Connor, M. (2000). Replaying the game: Hypnagogic images in normals and amnesiacs. *Science*, 290(5490), 350–353. https://doi.org/10.1126/science.290.5490.350

Tedeschi, R. G., & Calhoun, L. G. (1995). *Trauma and transformation.* SAGE.

Vollmer, J. (2010). *Schools cannot do it alone: Building support for America's public schools.* Enlightenment Press.

Whitaker, T., Whitaker, B., & Lumpa, D. (2008). Motivating and inspiring teachers: The educational leader's guide to building staff morale (2nd ed.). Routledge

Whitaker, T. (2020). What great teachers do differently: Nineteen things that matter most. New York: Routledge.

Wrzesniewski, A., McCauley, C., Rozin, P., & Schwartz, B. (1997). Jobs, careers, and callings: People's relations to their work. *Journal of Research in Personality*, 31(1), 21–33. https://doi.org/10.1006/jrpe.1997.2162

About the Author

Dan Butler serves as the principal of Epworth Elementary School in the Western Dubuque Community School District. Previously, he was the principal of Epworth and Farley Elementary Schools simultaneously for four years focusing on positive relationships with all members of the learning community, high impact instructional techniques, building leadership capacity in others, and establishing successful school cultures. Prior to serving as an administrator, Dan taught third and fifth grades in the Western Dubuque District, as well as serving as a baseball and football coach. In addition to his responsibilities as a building principal, Dan works as an adjunct professor in the Educational Leadership department at the University of Northern Iowa, where he earned his doctoral degree.

Dan has received numerous awards and most recently was recognized as a finalist for the School Administrators of Iowa Elementary Principal of the year in 2019 and 2020. He received the University of Northern Iowa Educational Leadership Legacy award in 2018 and was a 2017 bizTimes.biz Rising Star in the Dubuque area. For more than six years, Dan served as the co-moderator of Iowa Educational Chat (#IAedchat), a weekly Twitter forum dedicated to the latest trends in education. He has published various articles to Principal Magazine focused on digital leadership, literacy, productivity. and educator engagement. Dan and his wife, Johna, reside in Epworth with their two sons, Mason and Nolan. Read more about Dr. Butler by visiting danpbutler.com or follow him on Twitter: @danpbutler.

Presentations Available from Dan Butler

Dr. Dan Butler provides inspiring and motivating presentations, workshops, and customized professional learning opportunities. To book future speaking engagements, contact him at danpbutler@gmail.com or through various social media channels listed below.

Developing a Connected Mindset Through Intentional Practice
Understand how social media and web-based tools are used to enhance communication, improve public relations and personalized professional learning efforts, while fostering positive relationships.

Permission to be Great: Increasing Engagement in Your School
Investigate the research behind educator burnout and workplace engagement, while learning about strategies to excel in schools. This presentation will follow the framework outlined in Dan's book, *Permission to be Great.*

High Leverage Leadership: Strategies to Develop the Next Generation of Leaders
Learn simple, high-leverage strategies and routines to develop relationships, build leadership capacity, while empowering others.

Relationship-Driven Culture
Learn and apply six trauma-sensitive concepts to nurture a school culture driven by hope, resilience, and positive relationships.

Web: danpbutler.com
Twitter: @danpbutler
Instagram: @danpbutler
Voxer: @danpbutler

More from ConnectEDD Publishing

Since 2015, ConnectEDD has worked to transform education by empowering educators to become better-equipped to teach, learn, and lead. What started as a small company designed to provide professional learning events for educators has grown to include a variety of services to help teachers and administrators address essential challenges. ConnectEDD offers instructional and leadership coaching, professional development workshops focusing on a variety of educational topics, a roster of nationally recognized educator associates who possess hands-on knowledge and experience, educational conferences custom-designed to meet the specific needs of schools, districts, and state/national organizations, and ongoing, personalized support, both virtually and onsite. In 2020, ConnectEDD expanded to include publishing services designed to provide busy educators with books and resources consisting of practical information on a wide variety of teaching, learning, and leadership topics. Please visit us online at *connecteddpublishing.com* or contact us at: *info@connecteddpublishing.com*

Recent Publications:

Live Your Excellence: Action Guide by Jimmy Casas
Culturize: Action Guide by Jimmy Casas

Daily Inspiration for Educators: Positive Thoughts for Every Day of the Year by Jimmy Casas

Eyes on Culture: Multiply Excellence in Your School by Emily Paschall

Pause. Breathe. Flourish. Living Your Best Life as an Educator by William D. Parker

L.E.A.R.N.E.R. Finding the True, Good, and Beautiful in Education by Marita Diffenbaugh

Educator Reflection Tips Volume II: Refining Our Practice by Jami Fowler-White

Handle With Care: Managing Difficult Situations in Schools with Dignity and Respect by Jimmy Casas and Joy Kelly

Disruptive Thinking: Preparing Learners for Their Future by Eric Sheninger

Made in the USA
Monee, IL
21 June 2021